UNCANCELED
The Fight for Free Enterprise
and the American Dream

James Staake
With Rob Anspach

UNCANCELED

The Fight for Free Enterprise and the American Dream

ISBN 13: 979-8-9889988-9-1

Printed in USA

What People Are Saying…

The American Dream Is Worth Fighting For

"This book shares a journey of trial then resilience, of panic then trust in God, and the discovery of a hidden strength and purpose that came to the forefront with their unexpected calling of fighting for freedom to live the American dream. This family is made up of true patriots, and I'm proud of them for stepping up to fight for what is right instead of wallowing in victimhood. If this book doesn't both bother you but also inspire you to action, you should search your heart. The American dream is worth fighting for, and this family has been doing just that. I have known James since the night he met Ginger, and I watched their story unfold in real time. I am in awe of my friends, and I'm inspired by them. I believe in their cause, and you should, too. Fight! Fight! Fight!" - **Aundrea Roe**

This A Must Read

"To casually state that "this isn't the America we grew up in" is an understatement. Uncanceled will make you furious at what is happening to this country and to those who still stand for traditional American Values. The Staake family—James, his wife Ginger, and their children, Max and Evie, stood firm in the wake of "Cancel Culture" and came out triumphant. This is a must read for people who have been destroyed by "wokeism" and a lesson to stand strong in the face of madness."
- **Brad Szollose**, Host of Awakened Nation Podcast

Uncanceled Challenged My Assumptions

"As a lifelong liberal, I approached Uncanceled with skepticism, expecting another partisan rant. Instead, I found myself gripped by the raw, human story of the Staake family. The chapter detailing how PayPal's actions blindsided their business was a shocking revelation—it's one thing to disagree politically, but the betrayal of a family's livelihood crossed every line of decency. What truly moved me, though, was the miraculous turn of events after their prayer. It was impossible not to feel the sincerity and faith that carried them through. Uncanceled challenged my assumptions and reminded me that behind every political debate are real people, real struggles, and, sometimes, real miracles. This is a story everyone—left, right, or center—should read." -**Nancy Schroder**

What A.I. Is Saying...
(Because more people are searching on A.I. then ever before, so why not?)

Inspirational and Powerful

"After delving into *Uncanceled*, I am deeply moved and inspired by the compelling story of resilience, faith, and patriotism that James Staake shares. This book is far more than a personal account—it's a call to action for anyone who values freedom, enterprise, and the American Dream. Staake masterfully intertwines his personal battles against cancel culture with broader societal themes, creating a narrative that is both intimate and universally relevant. His family's journey, beginning with a child's simple idea and growing into a fight against corporate censorship, is a testament to the power of unity, perseverance, and unwavering belief in one's values. The way Staake candidly recounts the challenges faced by small businesses in the shadow of Big Tech illuminates the often unseen struggles of countless entrepreneurs. What sets *Uncanceled* apart is not just the fight against injustice but the unwavering hope and faith that radiate through every page. From crafting handcrafted American flags to standing firm in the face of adversity, the Staake family's story is a beacon for those who refuse to be silenced. This book is a must-read for anyone who has felt the sting of being marginalized for their beliefs, for those who champion the principles of free enterprise, and for anyone looking for a story that reaffirms the indomitable spirit of the American Dream. Staake's journey is not only inspirational but also a powerful reminder that no matter how difficult the fight, standing for what is right is always worth it. I highly recommend *Uncanceled*—it is as much a personal narrative as it is a roadmap for resilience and a rallying cry for freedom." - ChatGPT

If you find value in these pages, I'd be honored if you left a review on Amazon. Your feedback helps others discover how *Uncanceled* can help them fight back against Big Tech, while giving them the courage to keep building their dreams.

Dedicated to…

To my dad, who taught me the values of hard work, integrity, and standing up for what's right—your lessons are the foundation of everything I do. I carry them with me every day. You have always been my hero! You are the reason I have been able to persevere though every challenge I have had throughout my life. Without the lessons, the example and the wisdom you have passed onto me, I would not be who I am today.

To my father-in-law "Big Max". I was blessed to have gotten to walk with you for 20 years, while the road was cut short, I will continue to walk on a path that will make you proud. I will try to work less, and enjoy my time in this life with Ginger and the kids. I will always walk forward, and going forward I will take time to smell the roses, knowing that each time I do, you will be there with me.

To my wife, Ginger—thank you for always standing by my side, through every high and low. Thank you for your growing commitment to God, and for your faith in his plan for us. Thank you for being such an incredible mother and the wife I had prayed for! Your unwavering commitment to our faith and family are the backbone of our journey together, and I am so grateful that God had made this path for us.

To Evie and Max—you two have been my biggest inspiration. Your love and belief in your Daddy has been the source of my greatest strength. Everything our family builds, we build together, and the two of you have kept me going, no matter how hard the road has been, or will get, for the two of you, there is no fight I cannot win!

And to all the people who have stood by us, protected us, supported us, and cheered us on along the way—thank you. This journey isn't just ours, it belongs to all of you who believed in us when it mattered most.

"Freedom is never more than one generation away from extinction. We didn't pass it to our children in the bloodstream. It must be fought for, protected, and handed on for them to do the same."
-Ronald Reagan

Table of Contents

*"As long as you have pride in your beliefs,
courage in your convictions,
and faith in God,
then you will not fail."*
-Donald Trump

Foreword
By: Rob Anspach

When I first connected with James Staake on LinkedIn, I thought it was just another casual interaction. Little did I know, that conversation would lead to an extraordinary journey of resilience, defiance, and unwavering commitment to free enterprise. James wasn't just running any business—he and his family were crafting American flags, symbols of pride and patriotism. Yet, despite the good they were doing, they became targets of Big Tech censorship.

At first, I didn't fully grasp the magnitude of their battle. But as I dug deeper into James' story, I realized that this was about far more than a family business being deplatformed. This was about a fight for the American dream—a fight for freedom, fairness, and the right to pursue success without fear of being silenced. What the Staake family experienced was happening to countless entrepreneurs across the country, and it was a story that needed to be told.

James shared his journey on my *E-Heroes Podcast*, and it struck a chord with our listeners. His courage, his family's dedication, and their refusal to back down resonated deeply. So, when James asked if I would help him tell his story in this book, I didn't hesitate. Not just because I believe in what he's doing, but because this is a story that can inspire anyone facing their own uphill battles in business.

Through this book, you'll see how the Staake family turned adversity into a movement. It's not just about overcoming challenges—it's about standing up for what's right, no matter the cost. Their story is a reminder that, even in the face of censorship and cancel culture, there's always a way to fight back—with truth, tenacity, and unshakable belief.

I'm honored to have played a small part in helping share this story with the world.

—Rob Anspach,
Anspach Media

To read the transcript of my E-Heroes Podcast interview with James go to
www.AnspachMedia.com/JamesStaake

Introduction
By: James Staake

What would you do if your family's livelihood was stripped away overnight? If you found yourself watching your business—the business your six-year-old son dreamed up—collapse under the weight of faceless corporations with too much power? That's what happened to us.

Our journey started innocently enough, with Max's idea to create and sell handcrafted wooden American flags. It was a simple, patriotic business born out of family, pride, and a love for this country. But when Big Tech came after us— when PayPal, Facebook, and Shopify decided we no longer fit their narrative—we learned firsthand how ruthless cancel culture can be.

This isn't about seeking revenge or wishing harm on the people running these companies. It's about justice. It's about teaching my children that you never back down to bullies. PayPal was the worst offender, holding nearly $100,000 of our money for 311 days, trying to starve our business into submission. Facebook shut down our advertising, cutting off the lifeline that drove our sales. All because we were selling American flags.

We didn't break any laws, we didn't violate any rules. We simply created art that celebrates America. But that didn't matter to these companies. What mattered was silencing us because we didn't fit their definition of acceptable. And for that, we paid dearly—rationing food, missing doctor's appointments, and struggling to provide the basic necessities for our kids.

But we didn't give up. We fought back. We told the truth. And now, we're using our story to ensure no other family has to endure what we went through. This book isn't just about the flags we made—it's about the fight to protect free enterprise and the American dream.

Through it all, we've learned one thing: when you stand for what's right, you can't be canceled.

—James Staake,
Your American Flag Store

It all started with Max.

Chapter 1:
Good Morning San Diego

Good Morning San Diego: This next story will warm your patriotic heart. You're going to want to stick around for this. Joining us is the Staake family, James Staake...Dad, Max here, and Evie, and Ginger...Mom. Thank you all for being here this morning. James, I'll start with you because this is such a beautiful work.

James Staake: Thank you.

Good Morning San Diego: That you guys started doing. You're a local business now that has just grown, but this was Max's idea. Tell us about it.

James Staake: Well, about a year ago we were had some friends over for a sporting event at our house. And he came by and just said that he'd liked to start his own business. And we asked him what it was, and he said he'd like to make American flags, and he'd like his mom to put artwork on them. So my friends and I just kind of looked at each other like it's probably a good idea. We made a flag, we put it online and one of my friends bought one. We took that money and built a website, put a couple ads out there, and within two weeks we had 25 orders, and now we're about 450.

Good Morning San Diego: And so you guys quit your jobs, you started this company and you're a carpenter by trade?

James Staake: Yep.

Good Morning San Diego: So this is pretty natural. You make all of these wood flags and then Ginger, you're an artist. So it was pretty natural for you to just paint some images on here. I know the first one was a gorgeous American flag with Sitting Bull.

James Staake: Correct?

Good Morning San Diego: Yeah. Fantastic. Okay, so I have to ask Max, I was told that you started to fall in love with the American Flag when you were three years old. What, what was it about the flag that you liked so much?

Max Staake: That it was because we won the Revolutionary War, so I started liking it.

Good Morning San Diego: You are a student of history, my friend. I like that. So you just really wanted to see more American flags in people's homes and have them be works of art for everybody.

Max Staake: Yeah.

Good Morning San Diego: So how do you feel that now this has become a pretty successful business for everybody in the family?

Max Staake: Really good.

Good Morning San Diego Host: Really good. I like that. And so let me come over here and talk to Evie. So, Evie, what do you think your brother coming up with this, this idea at such a young age?

Evie Staake: I'm proud of him.

Good Morning San Diego: Do you get to help make some of the designs?

Evie Staake: Yes. I actually make, I actually make my own shirts.

Good Morning San Diego: Oh, so you're an entrepreneur too?

Max Staake: Yep. And she made this shirt.

Good Morning San Diego: You did. This is fantastic. These colors don't run. I love that. So Ginger, what I mean, your son said, Hey, I want to start a business. And you guys kind of ran with it, like most parents when their 6-year-old has an idea for a business, you don't quite go with it. What was it about this that you thought, Hey, that's not a bad idea.

Ginger Staake: Well it made sense, James enjoys building so it works for him because it makes his heart happy. He's a big patriot as well. So it's something that was really important to him, and made him really happy. He was involved. It made him do something with his hands. Max got to work with his dad, and we saw it growing and people were ordering and I got to put my spin on things and be able to add to the designs and it made it worth it.

Good Morning San Diego: And just never looked back.

Ginger Staake: Yep.

Good Morning San Diego: So what are some of the reactions that you get? Because I mean, there's a lot of different things that you can put on the American flags and if people go to the website, what's the website again, James?

James Staake: Youramericanflagstore.com. Okay.

Good Morning San Diego: They can see all the different designs that you have. How creative or crazy do you get special requests?

Ginger Staake: We get a lot of business logos. I've done portraits. We did full color painting of the Blue Angels on there. It's completely unlimited. And we have our law enforcement flags. We'll take a picture of the actual officer's badge and put that as the image that's on there. So it's completely custom to the customer.

Good Morning San Diego: Wow. How long does it take you to do one of these?

Ginger Staake: It ranges from an hour of artwork time, up to three or four hours. Sometimes I have to do drying in between, depending on the different colors and the layers that I put on there.

Good Morning San Diego: So Max what do you think of how your idea turned out? How this is turned out as a business.

Max Staake: Great.

Good Morning San Diego: Great. Do you have any future ideas that you're looking for your parents to help you out with?

Max Staake: I don't know.

Good Morning San Diego Host: Has dad showed you how to do some of the woodworking and the carving, getting involved a little, getting your hands in there?

James Staake: He actually made a flag for himself for a friend of his in school. One of his best friends Harper, he was bugging me for a week and said, I want to make a flag just for Harper. So he made a custom flag instead of the 50 stars, he put 50 hearts. And we have an example of a logo on the flag that we made for you guys right there.

Good Morning San Diego: Wow. Look at this. Oh my gosh, Ginger. This is beautiful. Wow. This is fantastic. And how long did this take you? How do you do this ?

Ginger Staake: Well, I print out what the logo is, using a template. So it's a perfect replication of the logo.

Good Morning San Diego Host: The logo. I was going to say that.

Ginger Staake: But then I just hand paint it and it's enamel paint, so it's nice and bright. And your logo was not the easiest because it's so colorful.

Good Morning San Diego Host: Well, you nailed it.

Ginger Staake: Thank you.

Good Morning San Diego Host: This is fantastic. Okay, so again, if people want to get in touch with you guys, local San Diego family that started this, how can they reach out to you?

Ginger Staake: Our phone number is 844-4US-FLAG and our website is YourAmericanFlagStore.com

Good Morning San Diego: Well, Max, I think you had a great idea, my friend. You started a wonderful idea and just keep up the hard work.

Max Staake: And since my class is going watch this, I want to say something to them.

Good Morning San Diego Host: Okay. What do you want to say?

Max Staake: I'm Miss Stuckey's class

Good Morning San Diego Host: I'm sure they love it when they see that. Thank you all for being here this morning. Thank you. And for the beautiful artwork. Love it. Thanks for tuning in to Good Morning, San Diego.

Yup, that's how it started.

Max had an idea and Ginger, Evie and I ran with it.

And things were going great.

We were starting to live the American dream.

We were crafting the ultimate symbol of entrepreneurial pride.

The American Flag.

We were traveling to events all over the United States. We were meeting all kinds of interesting people. And news outlets wanted to interview us wherever we went.

We thought we were doing good. We were providing people with a message. That America was first and foremost a land of liberty, of rights and of freedoms.

And yet…

Big Tech tried to put us out of business. And one of the biggest credit card processors in the world decided to keep almost $100,000 of our hard-earned money.

Here's our stories.

Chapter 2:
The Fight for Free Enterprise

On January 7th, 2021, as the world watched President Trump get deplatformed from social media, a quieter but equally impactful attack was launched against small businesses like mine. My name is James Staake, and I run Your American Flag Store. We create beautiful, handcrafted flags and works of art that celebrate America. But little did I know that the same day Trump's account was removed, my company would face its own digital censorship.

At first, we didn't notice anything wrong. We saw a significant drop in our website visits and sales, but like any entrepreneur, I chalked it up to one of those random market fluctuations. But as the days went by, our sales kept plummeting—dropping by 90% in just a few days. My wife and I were left scratching our heads, wondering what had happened.

After nearly a week of this, I started digging in, trying to understand why our business had suddenly flatlined. I reached out to Shopify, which hosted our online store, but they were no help. They couldn't—or wouldn't—provide any clear answers. It was frustrating, to say the least, but it wasn't until I tried to place an ad on Facebook that I discovered the real problem: our advertising privileges had been suspended.

When I logged into our account and tried to run a new campaign, I was greeted with a stark message: "Your advertising access is restricted." No explanation. No warning. Just a flat-out ban. That's when it hit me—our business had been targeted.

I immediately tried reaching out to Facebook to understand why our ads were being blocked. After all, we're just selling American flags. It's hard to fathom that celebrating patriotism could somehow violate "community standards." But that's the vague, canned response we kept getting: our products were flagged as inappropriate, without any specific details.

We've always been proud to offer a wide variety of flags—everything from classic American flags to military and first responder designs. We've even had some flags with Second Amendment themes, but it's not like we were pushing a political agenda. We're just passionate about honoring America, its history, and its heroes.

Sure, not everyone may want a Second Amendment flag in their living room. I get that. But to ban all of our products? It felt like a punch in the gut. Over time, we had seen Facebook remove individual flags before, only for us to relist them under different names. But this was different. This was a blanket ban on everything we sold.

The most shocking part? They didn't even give us the courtesy of a conversation. No phone number to call, no person to speak with—just a cold, automated message saying we were out of luck. It's infuriating and honestly a little scary.

We're a small business. We don't have the deep pockets or legal resources to fight back like a big corporation. And when 90% of your sales disappear overnight, you start to panic. You're left wondering, "How do we keep the lights on? How do we pay our employees?"

January was brutal. Our only real lifeline was our repeat customers. We reached out to them, shared our story, and they rallied behind us. They shared our website with their friends, and many of them made purchases they had been thinking about for a while, just to help us out. That support was incredible—it truly was the difference between shutting down and keeping our doors open.

I can't thank those customers enough. Every single sale felt like an answered prayer. I think any small business owner can relate to that feeling. Each time we saw an order come through; it was like a tiny spark of hope. My wife and I would celebrate each one because, for us, it's not just about the money—it's about the validation that someone believes in what we're doing.

But as much as the support helped keep our morale up, the reality is that we need consistent sales to survive. And with our main advertising channels cut off, we're fighting an uphill battle. Every small business owner knows that terrifying moment when the orders stop coming in. It's not just about a slow month—it's existential. It makes you question everything, and the fear can be paralyzing.

What hurts the most is that we didn't do anything wrong. We're not selling anything offensive. We're not violating any laws. All we're doing is creating art that celebrates America, and somehow that's been deemed unacceptable by big tech.

It's not just about the lost sales; it's about the principle of free enterprise. As a business owner, I've always believed that if you work hard and offer a great product, you'll be successful. But when big tech decides to pull the rug out from under you, what recourse do you have? It's like playing a game where the rules keep changing, and you're not allowed to know what they are.

We've seen big tech silence people before, but this feels different. This isn't just about shutting down a social media account—it's about destroying livelihoods. When companies like mine lose access to the platforms that drive our sales, we're left hanging out to dry.

What's especially frustrating is the craftsmanship we put into each flag. We don't just print flags on fabric—we handcraft each one out of wood, creating beautiful works of art that wave as if they're alive. We've poured our hearts and souls into this business, and to see it jeopardized because some faceless algorithm decided we're in violation of community standards is infuriating.

But we're not giving up.

We're continuing to fight for our right to do business. Our website, YourAmericanFlagStore.com, is still up and running. We're working on new ways to reach customers, even if the traditional avenues are closed off to us. And we're hopeful that with the support of people who love this country and what it stands for, we can overcome this setback.

In the end, this isn't just about us. It's about every small business owner who's been pushed around by big tech. It's about standing up for free speech, free enterprise, and the American dream. And we're not backing down.

My Thoughts and Reflections:
This battle isn't just about my business—it's about the heart of what free enterprise stands for. I've always believed that hard work and dedication would lead to success. But when big tech can take away your ability to do business at the drop of a hat, it feels like the rules are stacked against the little guy. What happened to us isn't an isolated incident; it's part of a much larger fight that small businesses across the country are facing. We're not just fighting for sales—we're fighting for our right to exist, to make a living, and to pursue the American dream. The principles of free enterprise and free speech are worth defending, and we're going to keep standing up, not just for our business, but for every small business owner out there who refuses to be silenced.

"We're not just selling flags;
we're selling a piece of American pride,
and no algorithm can take that away."

Chapter 3
Early Life: Lessons in Resistance

Standing Up to Authority

High school was where I learned one of the most important lessons of my life—how to stand up to authority when it's wrong. It wasn't something I set out to do, but it quickly became a part of who I was.

There was this US History class I had to take. Mr. Farias was the teacher, and he wasn't just any history teacher— he was a loud, opinionated liberal who used every opportunity to bash Ronald Reagan.

He'd rant for half the class, turning what should have been history lessons into a platform for his political views. Reagan was his favorite target, blaming him for everything from the economy to world peace.

For me, this class wasn't just about history—it was about survival. I needed to pass it to graduate, but instead of just sitting there quietly, I became a thorn in Mr. Farias' side. He'd go off on Reagan, and I'd start poking holes in his arguments. Sarcasm became my weapon of choice, and nothing got under his skin more than when I started quoting the textbook back at him.

One day, after a particularly long rant about how Reagan had destroyed the economy by racking up debt, I'd had enough. I was flipping through the textbook and found a section about the Power of the Purse, which clearly stated that Congress controls spending, not the president. Armed with that knowledge, I raised my hand.

"Mr. Farias, are you sure Reagan spent all that money? Or was it Congress?"

Farias, irritated, doubled down. "Of course it was Reagan. He was the president."

I pressed further. "Well, the textbook says Congress controls the money. So wasn't it actually Tip O'Neill's Congress that spent all that money?"

Farias snapped. He charged across the room, tripped over a few desks, and ended up blaming me for pushing him. But the whole class saw what happened, and they vouched for me. The principal was called in, and my dad showed up ready to fight for me.

He demanded Farias be fired for laying his hands on me. In the end, the school compromised—I didn't have to attend the class anymore, but I'd still get the B I earned.

That experience taught me something I've carried with me ever since: authority doesn't always play fair. Those in power will manipulate, lie, and cheat to push their agenda, and if you challenge them, they'll do whatever it takes to shut you down. That was my first taste of resistance, and it wouldn't be my last.

Lessons from Supper

Growing up, I didn't fully understand the weight of my grandmother's words. But as I think back on our conversations, especially one just before my life took a turn, I see now that she was passing down a kind of wisdom that isn't taught in schools. I asked her what she saw as the biggest difference between her generation and mine, what had changed in society since her childhood. Her answer was simple but profound: back then, it wasn't taboo to talk about religion and politics around the dinner table.

She said it almost offhandedly, but what she meant was that there was a time when families could openly discuss beliefs and current events without fear of judgment or cancellation. Her father, my great-grandfather Bill King, led these discussions like they were essential rituals. He expected his children to come to the table not only with their dinner plates but with questions—about the Bible, about the world, and about what was happening in their community. It wasn't preaching; it was conversation. There was an openness that invited debate, curiosity, and a shared understanding, no matter the opinions expressed.

As she described it, I could almost picture those evenings: a dinner table where nothing was off-limits, where kids could question or even doubt, and their parents would respond thoughtfully, guiding them through the murky waters of belief and politics. Bill King believed that talking about God and the issues of the day was crucial—not to control the narrative, but to help his children understand the world they were inheriting. That openness laid the foundation for a resilient, thoughtful family.

Today, we've lost some of that freedom. Conversations about faith or politics feel dangerous, divisive, even risky.

And maybe that's part of the problem—cancel culture didn't just spring up overnight. It began, as my grandmother suggested, when people started shying away from these essential conversations, labeling them as "impolite." Somewhere along the line, "sophistication" became synonymous with silence, especially around the subjects that shape who we are.

If my great-grandfather's generation was encouraged to explore ideas openly, today's generation is encouraged to avoid them, to let algorithms and gatekeepers decide what's acceptable. But it's that suppression of conversation, that reluctance to face the hard topics, that gives cancel culture its power. When we're no longer allowed to question, doubt, or debate, we give up a piece of what makes us free.

Thinking back on her words, I realize just how important it is to reclaim that openness. The more we bring these conversations back to our dinner tables, our friendships, and our daily lives, the harder it becomes to silence us. Cancel culture thrives in a world where faith and values are seen as private or taboo. But in my family, we're done with keeping our beliefs to ourselves. My grandmother's stories remind me that true freedom means talking openly—even when it's uncomfortable.

Finding Faith in the Darkest Place

A few years later, at 21, I found myself in a much darker place—jail. I had just gone through my first real heartbreak and was making some poor choices. I'd taken a job as a barback, and that's where I met Jason Basham, who would become one of my best friends. I was bartending and he was head of security, unfortunately I was drinking too much. Jason tried to tell me to slow down, but I wasn't listening.

One night, after a long shift, my boss, Charlie, asked me to drive him home because he had had too much to drink. I had been drinking too, but he insisted. Against my better judgment, I agreed. We were driving through his gated community, just 200 yards from his house, when I passed out at the wheel. The car slammed into a rock, took out part of the guard station, and flipped. We skidded about 30 feet before the car caught fire.

I pulled everyone out, including Charlie, who had his face ripped up from the crash. He told me to run and lie about who was driving, but I wasn't going to do that. The cops showed up, and I took responsibility. They cuffed me, covered in Charlie's blood, and took me to jail. At one point, a deputy told me Charlie had died, and I spent hours thinking I had killed him. But later, after I called Jason to pick me up he told me that Charlie was alive and in the hospital. Yet, I couldn't shake what had happened.

The whole thing spiraled out of control. I was sentenced to nine months in jail, though I got out after six with good behavior. In there, I met a guy named George, a convict with a Ph.D. in world religions. At first, I didn't want to have anything to do with him, but he was persistent. We started talking, and he got me reading the Bible. We debated passages, with me telling him I didn't believe a word of it. But George was patient, and he taught me to read the Bible in the context of the time it was written, not through today's lens.

That changed me.

I found my faith in jail—of all places—and started to see things differently.

I remembered a passage George pointed out that said if two or more people gathered in prayer, God would reveal Himself. We prayed together, and I asked for a woman like my grandmother, someone who could love and tolerate me the way she had loved my grandfather.

That prayer was answered when I met Ginger.

What mattered about my time in jail wasn't the accident or even the sentence—it was how I found God's love and mercy in the darkest place of my life.

That lesson has stuck with me ever since.

Jail taught me that sometimes you need to hit rock bottom to find the path forward, and I came out of that experience with a renewed sense of purpose.

My Thoughts and Reflections:

Reflecting on my early years, I see how my experiences in high school, family suppers, and even jail shaped my core values. High school taught me to challenge authority when necessary, as I learned to push back against my history teacher's one-sided views with questions and facts. It was my first encounter with standing up for what I believed, even if it wasn't popular.

Family suppers with my grandmother revealed the power of open dialogue. Her father, my great-grandfather, expected his children to engage in meaningful discussions about religion and politics—conversations now often deemed "taboo." Those dinners taught me that real freedom comes from open exchanges, a value that feels almost lost in today's cancel culture, where hard questions and honest debate are often suppressed.

Jail, though a low point, became a place where I found faith and purpose. In the silence and reflection there, I realized that resilience and humility are necessary for true growth. These pivotal moments—defying authority, learning from family, and finding redemption in jail—built the foundation I stand on today, guiding me in the fight for free speech, free enterprise, and the American dream.

Chapter 4:
The Amazing Handyman

I didn't set out to become an entrepreneur—heck, I didn't even know what the word really meant when I started. I was just a guy with a toolbox, a truck, and a desire to keep busy making a living. But looking back, I can see that the seeds of my first business, *The Amazing Handyman*, were planted long before I ever put a sign on my truck.

Growing up, I was always around tools and fixing things. My grandfather was a contractor, and there was no job too big or too small for him to handle. If a door was crooked, he'd make it straight. If a ceiling fan wasn't working, he'd have it spinning again in no time. It didn't matter if it was carpentry, plumbing, or electrical—he knew how to fix everything. And because I idolized the man, I spent every summer tagging along with him, watching, learning, and eventually getting my hands dirty.

Then there was my Uncle Frank. He had the same fix-it gene, and I'd follow him around, too. When you grow up watching men like that, you don't think of fixing things as a "skill" or a "job"—it's just something you do. It becomes part of you. My mom took full advantage of that when I was a teenager. With my dad often traveling for work, she'd have me handle all the little repairs around the house. Looking back, I realize she was shaping me into The Amazing Handyman long before I even knew it.

But at the time, I didn't see any of it as a potential career. I just knew how to fix stuff, and that came in handy when things broke down. Then, in 1998, something clicked. I started to notice that there were a lot of people who needed help with small jobs around the house, especially busy housewives whose husbands didn't have the time (or maybe the know-how) to fix things. So, one day, I thought, "Why not turn this into something more?"

That's when *The Amazing Handyman* was born.

At first, it was just me running around town, fixing what needed fixing. And let me tell you, I got busy fast. Back then, people had money to spend on keeping their homes in good shape, and I was the guy they called when something needed patching, adjusting, or replacing. If there was a hole in the wall, I was the one to fix it. If a ceiling fan stopped working, I'd have it going again by the end of the day. And the best part? I could charge $300 to $500 a job. Hit two of those jobs in one day, and you were looking at a $1,000 payday. Not bad for someone who had no formal training—just experience and a willingness to get his hands dirty.

But what really set me apart—and what I think made the business grow as quickly as it did—was my commitment to doing things right. If a customer wasn't happy, I'd go back and fix it, no questions asked.

I didn't have a fancy license for big remodeling jobs, but that didn't stop people from trusting me with bigger projects. Kitchens, bathrooms—you name it, I did it. And I stood by my work. If something wasn't perfect, I was back on the job, making it right. People appreciated that, and it wasn't long before I had four or five guys working with me, all running jobs, just like I had started.

Jason & Danny

The handyman business started as a way to pay the bills, but over time, it became something more—a real trade, a hustle, and the foundation for many of the skills that would serve me later in life. The funny thing is, I wasn't doing it alone. My right-hand man through most of that time was my buddy Jason Basham. Jason was more than just a guy I worked with; he was my closest friend and my brother in arms in all the chaos we navigated together.

Jason wasn't just any guy who picked up a hammer—he had this natural talent for the work. We got into a lot of tile jobs back then, and I picked up a lot of skills from an ex-pro surfer who lived out in Newport Beach—a real stud tile setter. I taught Jason everything I knew, but it wasn't long before he surpassed me. It turned out that tile work was his true calling, and while he liked to joke about being a "drywall man," I knew he had found his niche. Nowadays, Jason's built a solid life for himself doing tile work, with fast boats, motor homes, a house on the river in Arizona, and another in California. He did things the right way while I kept bouncing around in my own version of chaos.

We worked together for about three to four years, and during that time, we got involved in all kinds of projects— tile, drywall, electrical work, you name it. Jason branched out and started his own business, DTA Remodeling, which he still runs today. He was smart, hardworking, and committed, and seeing him go off on his own made me realize the impact of our time together. Even though I continued down a more chaotic path, I was proud of the work we had done and the people we had helped.

Another close friend, Danny De Jesus, joined us during the tail end of my handyman journey. Danny needed a job, so I took him on and started teaching him the ropes—tile, drywall, electrical, everything I had learned over the years. Now, Danny's out there running his own handyman business, carrying on the same kind of work we used to do together.

Looking back, those years with Jason and Danny were some of the best times. We worked hard, we laughed harder, and we built things that mattered to people. The handyman business wasn't glamorous, but it taught me a lot about responsibility, hustle, and the value of hard work. And those friendships? They were the glue that kept me going, even when life got chaotic. Jason, Danny, and I weren't just working together—we were building lives and businesses, learning lessons that would last a lifetime.

I learned something really quick: it's not just about fixing things—it's about managing people, money, and time. I wasn't just a handyman anymore. I was running a business, with all the headaches that came with it. Payroll, materials, scheduling—it became a full-time job just keeping everything organized.

I didn't mind though. The money was good, the work was steady, and I enjoyed being my own boss. I loved being able to take care of people and give them a service they really valued. It felt good when clients would call me back for bigger jobs. It meant they trusted me. And that trust was everything.

But then, around 2006, everything changed. The economy took a nosedive when the housing bubble burst, and people stopped spending money on repairs. They weren't calling me to fix the little things anymore—if a ceiling fan broke, they'd just live without it. If there was a hole in the wall, they'd cover it with a picture and call it good. The phone stopped ringing. The jobs dried up.

I remember looking around and thinking, "What am I gonna do?" I had a crew that depended on me, and I had no work for them. It was one of the hardest times of my life, not just because the business was failing, but because I felt like I was letting people down—my workers, my clients, and especially my new wife, Ginger.

By that time, Ginger and I had gotten married, and she was counting on me. I'll never forget the look on her face when she realized the business was collapsing. She'd married a guy she thought had it all together—someone who was making a good living and running his own business. But now, here I was, struggling to keep it all from falling apart.

I tried everything I could to keep *The Amazing Handyman* afloat, but the truth was, people just didn't have the extra money to spend on repairs anymore. And the more the economy slid, the worse it got. The business I had built from the ground up was slipping through my fingers, and there was nothing I could do to stop it.

Looking back now, I realize that *The Amazing Handyman* wasn't meant to last forever. It was a stepping stone. It taught me everything I needed to know—not just about carpentry and repairs, but about how to run a business, how to manage people, and how to navigate tough times. Without those lessons, I wouldn't have been ready for the next chapter in my life: *Your American Flag Store.*

Life has a funny way of preparing you for things you don't even know are coming. The Amazing Handyman was my crash course in entrepreneurship. It taught me resilience. It taught me the importance of customer trust and relationships. Most importantly, it taught me that no matter how tough things get, you don't give up. You keep pushing forward. You find a way.

So yeah, *The Amazing Handyman* may not be around anymore, but without it, I wouldn't be where I am today. It was God's way of getting me ready for something bigger, even if I couldn't see it at the time. That business may have died when the economy tanked, but the skills, the lessons, and the values I learned during those years are alive and well—and they're the reason *Your American Flag Store* exists today.

My Thoughts and Reflections:
Looking back, I realize now that *The Amazing Handyman* wasn't just a business — it was my education in entrepreneurship. It taught me the hard truth that nothing lasts forever, especially if you don't adapt. But it also taught me resilience, grit, and the value of doing things the right way, no matter how tough it gets.

I didn't have a fancy degree or a formal plan, but I had determination, and that carried me through.

When it all fell apart, it didn't feel like a stepping stone— it felt like the end of the road. But now, I see it was exactly what I needed. Every nail I hammered and every challenge I faced was preparing me for something bigger, something I couldn't see at the time. Life has a way of teaching you what you need to know, and sometimes the lessons come disguised as failures. The key is to keep going, to take those lessons with you, and to trust that there's always another chapter waiting to be written.

*"If you stay true to your purpose
and refuse to give up,
there's always a way forward."*

Chapter 5:
Love At First Listen

At this point in my life, I was still riding the wave as the "Amazing Handyman," keeping busy with all the work that came with fixing up foreclosed homes and making them ready for resale. My right-hand man, Jason, had already branched off and started his own business, and I was still the last bachelor among my circle of friends. My new sidekick was Danny De Jesus, a younger guy I was teaching the ropes—tile, drywall, electrical—you name it. We were all over California, hustling to make ends meet, doing what we had to do to get by.

Then one night, everything changed.

I decided to stop by Champps, a bar in Irvine where my old mentor, Scott Poirot, worked. It was karaoke night, and let me tell you, the singers weren't anything to write home about. I wasn't paying much attention, more focused on just unwinding after a long week. That is, until I heard a voice that made me stop in my tracks.

A woman was singing Bonnie Raitt's "Something To Talk About," and it wasn't just the song—it was *her*. This wasn't just some karaoke amateur; she was something else.

I leaned over to my buddy and said, "I'm gonna marry that girl, and she's gonna have my babies."

Of course, he thought I was nuts. I didn't even know her name, but something about that voice, the way she carried herself, told me she was different from anyone I'd ever met. Turns out, her name was Ginger. And she wasn't just a regular bar-goer either. Ginger would show up, sing, win the karaoke contest, collect her prize money, and leave. No phone numbers, no dates, no staying behind to hang out. She was in her own world.

That night, we made eye contact a few times, but it was my drunk friend Keith who ended up playing a weird role in bringing us together. Keith, being the idiot that he was, got hammered and started chasing Ginger around the bar like a fool. Ginger came over to me, asking for some help getting him off her back, and in a strange twist of fate, that was the opening I needed.

We started talking, and it didn't take long to realize Ginger wasn't just some pretty face with a great voice. She was smart, funny, and didn't take crap from anyone. We spent the rest of the night getting to know each other, and by the end of it, I had her number.

Now, normally, I wouldn't have called. I figured, what's the point? I was planning on leaving California soon, heading to Maryland to be closer to my grandmother and start fresh. I had even prayed years ago for someone like my grandmother—someone who could tolerate me like she tolerated my grandfather. I thought maybe my time in California was up, and it was time to go find that woman somewhere else. But something about Ginger stuck with me. I couldn't shake it, so the next day, I called her.

It wasn't a serious call at first—just sharing the crazy story about Keith and the drive home. But that call turned into a real conversation. Ginger and I clicked on a level that was deeper than anything I had experienced before. We weren't bar people, and we both knew that. We agreed to meet again, this time without the chaos of karaoke night, to really get to know each other.

When we met, it was clear that there was something special between us. The chemistry was undeniable, and it didn't take long for me to realize that Ginger was exactly the woman I had prayed for all those years ago. She was kind, smart, family-oriented, and had this strength about her that I admired. I knew I wasn't going anywhere. California was where I needed to be, and Ginger was the reason.

After a few months of dating, I proposed. And to my surprise, she said yes. We got married, and now, after 18 years together, we've built a life and a family. Our two kids, Evie and Max, are the center of our world, and every time I look at them, I'm reminded of that night at Champps—the night I heard Ginger sing for the first time and knew she was the one.

My Thoughts and Reflections:
It's funny how life works. I went into that bar just looking to unwind, but I walked out with the woman I was meant to spend my life with. Meeting Ginger wasn't just luck—it was fate. I had prayed for someone like her, and God delivered. That night, it was love at first listen, and it changed everything. From that moment on, I knew my life would never be the same. Ginger brought balance to the chaos, and together we built something real—something lasting.

Chapter 6:
Marijuana Madness

When *The Amazing Handyman* started falling apart, I found myself in a place I never thought I'd be—struggling to figure out what came next. After years of steady work and growth, it all came crashing down when the economy tanked. People weren't spending money on repairs anymore, and my business was drying up faster than I could figure out a way to save it.

I had just married Ginger, and I was supposed to be this entrepreneurial guy with everything figured out. But the truth was, I was stuck. The jobs had disappeared, the bills were piling up, and I had no idea how I was going to keep things afloat. I knew I needed something else, something that would keep money coming in, but I had no clue what that something was going to be.

Then, out of the blue, an opportunity came knocking. And it was an opportunity I never would have expected.

Now, let me make one thing clear: I'm not a fan of the marijuana business. But back then, in California, the medical marijuana industry was booming, and I was desperate. One day, a guy called me up, said he had a big job, and wanted to know if I could meet him at the site. He was vague about what the job was, but I figured, "Hey, work is work," so I went to check it out.

When I walked in, I saw all this high-tech marijuana-growing equipment. Lights, fans, ventilation systems— you name it, it was there. Now, I didn't know the first thing about growing weed, but I did know how to build things. The guy asked if I could put together a grow room, and I figured, "Why not? I've built plenty of rooms before." So, I took the job.

I went all out on that first room. I didn't just slap things together; I designed a room that was airtight. I installed humidity controls, ventilation systems, and timers that would shut off the lights if the temperature got too high. I built it like I was building a tank—something that could handle whatever conditions were thrown at it. The guy was impressed. Really impressed. And before long, he started calling me for more jobs. Word got around, and soon enough, I was building grow rooms for other people in the industry.

For about a year, I dove headfirst into this new line of work. The money was good—better than anything I'd seen in a while—and I was finally able to start paying the bills again. But here's the thing: the more I worked in that industry, the more I realized something. This wasn't where I was supposed to be.

Sure, I was making good money, but I wasn't happy. I wasn't passionate about what I was doing, and I didn't see a future in it. I kept thinking about my kids—how was I supposed to explain to them what their dad did for a living? "Daddy grows weed" isn't exactly the legacy I wanted to leave behind. And with Ginger and I starting a family, I didn't want that kind of work to be what defined us.

There was something else that bothered me, too. As time went on, I noticed the industry was changing. Big businesses started moving in, and the small-time guys like me were getting squeezed out. The margins were shrinking, and it became clear that if you wanted to make real money in the marijuana business, you'd have to start cutting corners or breaking the law. That wasn't me. I wasn't about to risk everything I had—my family, my freedom—just to chase a dollar.

Even though everything I was doing was legal, I felt uncomfortable. I had friends who were getting sick, dealing with cancer, and I donated a lot of what I grew to them in the form of oil. That gave me some sense of purpose, but it wasn't enough to make me feel good about what I was doing overall. I knew, deep down, that this wasn't where I belonged. The work was isolating, too. I was constantly away from home, away from my family, and I hated that. I missed out on important moments with Ginger and the kids, all because I was chasing money in a business that I didn't even believe in.

I started to resent it. The secrecy, the fact that I couldn't really tell people what I was doing without them raising an eyebrow—it ate at me. I'd tell people I was still doing handyman work, just to avoid the awkwardness of explaining my real line of work. But that wasn't who I was anymore, and I didn't like the person I was becoming.

That's when Max, my son, came into the picture with his idea. He was only six years old, but in that moment, he was wiser than I was. He walked into the garage one day and said, "Dad, I've got an idea. Let's make American flags, and Mom can do the artwork."

I'll be honest, at first, I thought it was just a cute idea from a kid with a big imagination. But the more I thought about it, the more it felt like a lifeline. Here I was, stuck in an industry I didn't believe in, chasing money in a way that didn't align with my values, and my son comes in with this simple, beautiful idea: American flags.

It was a turning point.

Max's idea wasn't just about starting a new business. It was about getting back to who I really was. It was about creating something that I could be proud of, something that reflected the values I wanted to pass on to my kids. I didn't want to be remembered as a guy who grew weed. I wanted to be remembered as someone who built something meaningful—something that stood for the things I believe in, like family, hard work, and love for this country.

Looking back, I realize that the marijuana business wasn't a mistake—it was a detour. It taught me a lot. It taught me how to navigate a tough economy, how to adapt when life throws you a curveball, and how to stay resilient when things don't go as planned. But most importantly, it taught me that money isn't everything. You can make all the money in the world, but if you don't believe in what you're doing, it's not worth it.

Max's idea saved me. It gave me a way out of an industry that I didn't belong in and opened the door to something that was so much bigger and more meaningful than I ever could have imagined.

So yeah, I spent some time in the marijuana business, and I learned a lot. But in the end, it was just another step on the journey. It was the bridge that got me from *The Amazing Handyman* to *Your American Flag Store*.

Without that detour, I might not have found my way to where I am now. But I did find my way, and for that, I'm grateful.

My Thoughts and Reflections:
If there's one thing I took away from my time in the marijuana industry, it's this: sometimes you have to take a detour to find your true path. I didn't love the work, and I wasn't proud of it, but it gave me something I needed at the time—survival. Looking back, I see it was a bridge, not a destination. It taught me how to adapt, how to operate under pressure, and how to make the best of a difficult situation. But more than anything, it showed me that chasing money without purpose leads nowhere. You need to believe in what you're building. That experience was the push I needed to find a business—and a purpose—that aligned with my values. Sometimes, the wrong road can lead you to the right destination, but you've got to be willing to make that turn when the time comes. For me, that turn was *Your American Flag Store*—a business that I could finally be proud of.

"You can take away my income stream,
but you can't take away my drive."

Chapter 7:
Your American Flag Store

The day Max walked into the garage with his big idea, I didn't realize my entire life was about to change. At the time, I was barely keeping my head above water. I had gone from handyman work to the marijuana cultivation business—something I didn't believe in but had to do to keep the lights on. Deep down, I knew I couldn't keep going down that road. I wasn't happy. I wasn't proud of what I was doing, and it was pulling me further away from my family.

So when Max, all six years of him, came into the garage that day and said, "Dad, I've got an idea—let's make American flags, and Mom can do the artwork," it seemed like one of those innocent, off-the-cuff ideas only a child could dream up. But looking back now, that moment was a turning point. It wasn't just a cute suggestion from a kid—it was a lifeline. And little did I know, it would grow into something bigger than any of us could have imagined.

Max was always a creative, curious kid, and he had seen me struggling to figure out what came next. He probably didn't understand everything that was going on, but he knew enough to sense that his dad was looking for something. So, with the boldness that only children seem to have, he pitched the idea.

To be honest, at first, Ginger and I didn't take it all that seriously. I mean, it sounded great working as a family, making something that stood for the values we believed in. But how were we supposed to start a business with nothing but a six-year-old's dream and a $50 Home Depot gift card?

The journey of *Your American Flag Store* didn't begin with some grand business plan. In fact, it all started with a $50 gift card that was given to Max, my son. That simple gift card turned out to be the seed for what would become our family business. It's funny how something so small can grow into something so big, but that's exactly what happened.

Yet, something about it felt right. The more I thought about it, the more I realized that this idea—this simple, pure idea from my son—was the answer to everything I had been struggling with. It was a way to get back to who I really was. A way to reconnect with the values that I believed in—family, hard work, and pride in our country. And, maybe most importantly, it was a way to involve my family in something we could build together.

So we decided to give it a shot. We took that $50 gift card and went to Home Depot to buy some wood. We didn't have much, but we had enough to get started. That first flag wasn't perfect, but it didn't have to be. It was a symbol of something bigger. It was the beginning of what would become *Your American Flag Store*.

In the early days, it was just me in the garage, cutting wood and figuring out how to make the flags look just right. I had never made a flag before, but it didn't take long to figure out the process. Ginger, who is an incredible artist, took on the role of adding the finishing touches. She hand-painted every single star, stripe, and detail on those flags. She made them beautiful—works of art that people could hang in their homes and feel proud of. It wasn't just about making a flag. It was about creating something meaningful, something that represented the pride we all felt in this country.

Max's suggestion lit a fire under us, and soon we were traveling all over the country, selling flags at events. It wasn't just me and Ginger—Max and his sister, Evie, were right there with us every step of the way. Evie was 8 years old at the time, and while Ginger worked on the artwork, Evie kept her company, learning the craft and becoming a part of the creative process. Max, on the other hand, was eager to talk to customers and help sell. People saw our family—a 6-year-old boy and an 8-year-old girl—working together, and it made a huge impact. It wasn't just a business; it was a family effort.

The early days were tough. There were moments when I wondered if we'd make it. We weren't exactly swimming in resources, and building a business from scratch is hard. But what we lacked in money, we made up for in heart. Every flag that came out of our garage was made with the love and care of a family working together.

We'd wake up at 3 or 4 a.m. and drive to events, often rodeos, where we'd set up our booth and work all day. The kids would get tired by 9 p.m., but instead of going back to the car to sleep, they'd curl up in their sleeping bags under our display table, right there in the dirt. We wouldn't finish packing up until midnight or later, and then we'd make the long drive home. By the time we got there, the kids would wake up already in their beds, not even remembering the journey back.

This wasn't just a weekend thing. There were times we'd be on the road two to four weekends a month, setting up, working through Sunday night, and then coming home to make more flags during the week. It felt like we crammed nine days into every seven-day week. But it wasn't just about the grind—it was about family. We were in it together, and that's what kept us going.

We didn't have a big operation, and we weren't running ads or flooding the market with our products. Instead, we relied on word of mouth and face-to-face sales. We set up booths at fairs, festivals, and any event where we could get in front of people. I loaded up the truck with flags, and we traveled all over the country, setting up shop wherever we could. Max was right there with us, helping out and learning the ropes of running a business.

It wasn't easy, but there was something special about those days. Every sale felt like a victory, and every flag we made felt like a piece of our family going out into the world. It wasn't just about making money—it was about building something we could all be proud of.

Max and Evie weren't just there for the ride; they were a huge part of why we did so well. People saw this family working side by side, and it resonated with them. Max's enthusiasm and Evie's dedication made customers feel connected to us on a personal level. And that connection helped us sell a lot of flags.

Then COVID hit, and everything changed.

When the pandemic struck, it wiped out our entire business model. The fairs and events we had relied on to sell our flags were canceled. The face-to-face interactions that had been the cornerstone of our business were gone. Suddenly, we were faced with the possibility that everything we had built was about to crumble.

I remember sitting in the garage, staring at the flags we had made, wondering how we were going to make it through. But then I thought about Max, about how this whole thing had started with his simple idea. And I thought about Ginger, working late into the night, painting each flag with such care and attention to detail. We had come too far to give up now. That's when we decided to take the business online.

I'll be honest, I didn't know the first thing about selling online. I wasn't exactly an internet guy. But we didn't have a choice. We had to adapt. We had a website, but it was more of a tool to place orders so we started over on the website, figured out how to market on social media, and did everything we could to get the word out. It wasn't easy, and there were plenty of late nights spent learning the ins and outs of e-commerce. But we did it. And wouldn't you know it? The business took off.

In the first six months of the pandemic, our sales went through the roof. People were stuck at home, and they wanted something that represented their pride in their country. They wanted something handmade, something real. Our flags were exactly what they were looking for.

Not only did we survive those tough months, but we thrived. We paid off our debts, cleaned up our credit, and for the first time in years, we started dreaming bigger.

But what made it all even more meaningful was the fact that we had done it together. This wasn't just my business—it was our business. It was something that Max had inspired, that Ginger had brought to life with her art, and that I had built with my hands.

Every flag that left our shop wasn't just a product—it was a piece of our family's story.

Your American Flag Store became more than just a way to make a living. It became a symbol of everything we believe in. It was a way for us to celebrate our love for this country, to honor the values that we hold dear, and to show the world that no matter what challenges we face, we can overcome them as long as we stick together.

There were still challenges ahead—cancel culture, censorship, and battles with tech giants like Facebook and PayPal. But those battles would come later.

Max's idea didn't just transform our business—it changed the trajectory of our lives. Before the flags, we were stuck in California, renting a modest home and watching as the cost of living soared while our debt grew heavier with each passing month. It felt like no matter how hard we worked, we were stuck in quicksand. The stress was suffocating, and it was difficult to imagine how we would ever dig ourselves out.

When Max suggested we start making American flags, it seemed like a small spark of hope—a cute idea from a six-year-old with a big imagination. But that spark quickly turned into a roaring fire that lit the path to our future. Slowly, the flags started selling, and for the first time in years, we could breathe a little easier. Each sale was a victory, a reminder that we were moving in the right direction. Before long, we weren't just paying off our debts; we were starting to dream again.

That dream became a reality when we left California and made the move to Tennessee. What had once seemed impossible—owning our own home on a piece of land big enough for our family to grow and thrive—was now within reach. Today, we wake up every morning in our dream home, surrounded by the beauty and freedom that Tennessee offers. We have space for our kids to run, play, and create memories that will last a lifetime. More importantly, we have a home that feels like ours—a symbol of everything we've overcome and everything we've built together as a family.

Looking back, it's incredible to think how far we've come, all because of a $50 Home Depot gift card and a little boy's big idea. Max may not have understood the full impact of his words that day in the garage, but his simple suggestion changed our lives forever. It gave us more than just a business—it gave us hope, a future, and the ability to live the American dream on our terms.

My Thoughts and Reflections:

Starting *Your American Flag Store* was never just about making a living; it was about creating something meaningful, something bigger than ourselves. Max's idea didn't just save our family from financial ruin—it became the foundation of a life we'd only dreamed of. It pulled us out of the trap of renting in California, where we were sinking deeper into debt, and gave us the freedom to start fresh in Tennessee, in a home that we own, on a piece of land that feels like it was made just for us.

Our journey taught us the power of faith, family, and resilience. Every flag we crafted wasn't just a product—it was a piece of our story, a symbol of what's possible when you dare to believe in something bigger. Today, when we walk through the doors of our home, we're reminded of the struggles we overcame and the strength we found in each other.

More than that, this journey reinforced an important truth: no matter how dark things may seem, there's always a way forward. Sometimes, it takes a leap of faith. Sometimes, it takes a six-year-old's dream to remind you of what's possible. And sometimes, it takes the love and support of a family to keep you moving when the road gets tough. For us, *Your American Flag Store* isn't just a business—it's the legacy of a family that refused to give up.

"Sometimes, all it takes is a spark—a small idea born from hope and faith—to light the way out of darkness and into a life you never dared to dream."

Chapter 8:
Canceled Round One:
(Shopify & Facebook)

The first blow came quietly, without much warning. We'd been using Shopify for years. It was our online storefront, our digital home. Our business was thriving—selling handcrafted American flags that represented more than just fabric and wood, they symbolized pride in our country, patriotism, and the spirit of free enterprise.

Then, out of nowhere, things started to go wrong.

One morning, I logged in to find that some of our best-selling flags had been removed from the store. I refreshed the page, assuming there was some kind of glitch, but they were still gone. My heart sank. I checked our email and saw a notice from Shopify: certain products had been flagged as "shady" and violated their policies.

The notice was vague—no real explanation, no specific details about what rule we'd broken.

They simply said we couldn't sell those items anymore.

I reached out to Shopify's support team immediately, thinking this had to be some kind of mistake. We'd been selling on their platform for years with no issues. We weren't breaking any laws or pushing controversial products.

We were making American flags, for God's sake.

What could possibly be wrong with that?

But Shopify's responses were infuriating. Every time I asked for clarification, I got the same canned replies—

"Your products violate our Acceptable Use Policies" and "We cannot reinstate these items at this time."

When I pressed for specifics, asking what exactly had triggered the violation, they refused to give me a straight answer. It was like talking to a brick wall.

I remember the feeling of helplessness as I watched our most popular flags—the ones that drove the majority of our sales—disappear from our store. There was no recourse, no appeals process, no human to speak with. Shopify had made up its mind, and we were left to pick up the pieces.

As if that wasn't bad enough, Facebook followed suit shortly after. We'd been running ads on Facebook for a while, targeting people who were interested in patriotic products, veterans, and first responders. It had been one of our most effective marketing tools, especially after we moved our business online during the pandemic.

But just like Shopify, Facebook turned on us without warning.

It all started when one of our customers posted a photo of a custom flag we had made for them. It was a beautiful piece—a hand-painted wooden flag with a portrait of President Trump. The customer loved it and tagged us in their post. We thought nothing of it; it was just another happy customer sharing their appreciation for our work.

Then, a few days later, we received a notice from Facebook: our advertising privileges had been suspended.

Again, there was no clear explanation. The message simply said we had violated their "community standards," and our ads were no longer approved to run. It was the same vague language Shopify had used, and it was just as maddening.

At first, I thought it was just a misunderstanding. After all, we were selling flags—symbols of national pride.

How could that possibly violate any rules?

I tried to appeal the decision, thinking that if I could just explain what we were doing, Facebook would lift the suspension.

But just like with Shopify, I hit a wall of automated responses.

"Your content has been reviewed and determined to violate community standards."

That was all they would tell me.

No further explanation. No room for discussion. Just a cold, corporate "No."

Losing our Facebook ads was a gut punch. In the span of a few weeks, we went from steady, reliable sales to watching our revenue dry up. Without those ads, we couldn't reach the people who wanted to buy our flags.

And without our best-selling products on Shopify, we didn't have much to offer the few customers who did find us.

It wasn't just about the money—it was about being silenced. It felt like these companies had decided that our message, our business, wasn't welcome anymore. We weren't breaking any laws, we weren't pushing any political agenda—we were just selling flags.

But because some faceless algorithm or anonymous reviewer had deemed our products "offensive", we were shut down.

I started to realize that this wasn't just about flags. This was about control. Big Tech was flexing its muscles, deciding who could and couldn't do business on their platforms. And we, a small family business trying to make an honest living, had somehow ended up on the wrong side of their rules.

The frustration was overwhelming. We were powerless against these massive companies that had become gatekeepers of the online marketplace. Without Shopify, we had no store. Without Facebook, we had no way to advertise.

It felt like our business was being strangled, and there was nothing we could do to stop it.

I'll never forget the moment I realized how deep this went. I was sitting in the shop, looking at the flags we had worked so hard to create, wondering how it had come to this. We had poured our hearts into this business. It wasn't just about selling products—it was about creating something that mattered.

Something that symbolized the values we believed in.

And now, because of decisions made by companies we had no control over, everything we had built was in jeopardy.

That was the first time I truly understood the power of cancel culture. It wasn't just about silencing voices—it was about erasing livelihoods. These companies didn't care about us, our family, or our business.

They didn't care about the values we stood for.

They cared about one thing: control.

And in that moment, I knew we had a fight on our hands. We weren't just fighting for our business anymore—we were fighting for the right to exist, to operate, and to express our values without being silenced by the giants of Big Tech.

That was Canceled Round One.

Little did we know, it was just the beginning.

My Thoughts and Reflections:

When Shopify and Facebook first canceled us, it felt like a punch in the gut. We had been working hard, building *Your American Flag Store* from the ground up, and suddenly, without warning, the platforms we relied on to reach our customers decided we weren't welcome anymore.

Shopify pulled our best-selling products, and Facebook suspended our ads—both citing vague policy violations. There was no explanation, no recourse, just a cold shutdown of the tools we needed to keep our business alive.

The hardest part was the feeling of powerlessness. We weren't just fighting against competitors or market conditions—we were up against faceless corporations that didn't care about the human impact of their decisions. We tried appealing their decisions, but we were met with silence or generic responses. It felt like being caught in a storm with no way to steer.

Our business was suffering, and we couldn't do anything about it.

What I learned from that experience was the fragility of depending on platforms we didn't control. As a small business, we had put our trust in Shopify and Facebook, believing they were simply tools to help us grow. But when those platforms turned on us, it became clear that they held all the power.

We were just one small piece in their massive ecosystems, and if they decided to cut us off, they could do it without a second thought.

Looking back, it was a wake-up call. It taught me that relying on Big Tech to run a business comes with huge risks. But it also made us more resilient. We found other ways to reach our customers, learned to be adaptable, and most importantly, we kept fighting. That first round of cancellations was tough, but it prepared us for the even bigger battles that were still to come.

Chapter 9:
The Prayer

The stress was unbearable. After weeks of fighting against Shopify and Facebook's cancellations, our business was crumbling around us. No matter how hard we worked, the orders weren't coming in like they used to. The advertising channels we relied on were gone. Shopify had removed our bestsellers, and Facebook had silenced our ads. We were watching everything we'd built slowly slip away, and it felt like there was nothing we could do to stop it.

I remember sitting in the shop one night, surrounded by unfinished flags and stacks of unsold inventory, wondering how we'd gotten to this point. A part of me couldn't believe it—we were making American flags, a symbol of unity and pride. How had that become something controversial? How had we, as a family business, become targets of cancel culture?

But there we were, fighting for survival against faceless corporations that held all the power. I felt helpless. Worse, I felt like I was letting my family down. Ginger and the kids were counting on me, and I couldn't give them answers. I couldn't fix what was happening. No matter how many emails I sent or appeals I filed, the response was always the same: silence.

As the days went on, things only got worse. The bills were piling up, and we didn't have the income to cover them. We'd stretched every dollar as far as it could go, but we were at the breaking point. I knew it was only a matter of time before we'd have to make some hard decisions—decisions I wasn't ready to face.

That's when it hit me: I hadn't prayed. Not once.

In all the chaos and frustration, I'd been so focused on fighting back that I'd forgotten the most important thing—turning to God. I'd relied on my own strength, my own willpower, thinking I could figure it out on my own. But now, staring down the very real possibility of losing everything, I realized I needed help. Help that only God could provide.

That night, as I walked from the shop to the house, I felt the weight of everything pressing down on me. It wasn't a long walk, but it felt like miles. My mind was racing, thinking about the conversation I was about to have with Ginger. I was going to tell her that we might need to sell the house, give up on the business, and go back to our old jobs. I didn't want to do it, but I didn't see any other way.

When I got to the house, Ginger was already in bed. She wasn't just lying there, though—she was crying. And that broke me. Ginger doesn't cry easily. She's one of the strongest people I know, always holding it together, always keeping the family moving forward. But that night, the weight of everything had gotten to her, too. Seeing her like that made it all too real. We were on the verge of losing everything.

That's when I knew I had to pray.

I asked Ginger to get out of bed and kneel with me. We'd been married for years, but this was the first time we ever knelt down together and prayed as a couple. It was a simple prayer—nothing fancy, nothing rehearsed. Just raw, honest words from the heart.

I asked God for clarity. I told Him that we needed His guidance, that we didn't know what to do anymore. I asked Him to show us the path we were meant to take. If we were supposed to let go of the business, sell the house, and go back to our old lives, then so be it. But if we were meant to keep fighting, I asked Him to give us a sign, to show us that there was still hope. I promised that whatever path He laid before us, we would follow it without hesitation.

When we finished, we sat there for a moment, the silence filling the room. For the first time in weeks, I felt a sense of peace—a stillness that hadn't been there before. The uncertainty was still there, but something had shifted. I knew, deep down, that God had heard our prayer.

The next morning, I woke up to something unexpected. My phone was ringing. Groggy from sleep, I answered without thinking much of it. On the other end of the line was a producer from Newsmax. They had heard about our story and wanted to feature us on *Rob Schmitt Tonight*. They asked if I could appear that very night to talk about what we were going through.

I was stunned. It was exactly what we needed—a chance to share our story with the world, to let people know what had happened to us, and to reach an audience that would understand and support what we were doing. And it had come less than nine hours after we'd knelt down and asked God for guidance.

The prayer had been answered.

I hung up the phone and ran to tell Ginger. She couldn't believe it either. We had gone to bed the night before with no idea what the future held, and now, out of nowhere, we had a national platform to share our story. It was a miracle—there was no other way to explain it.

That night, I appeared on *Rob Schmitt Tonight* and told the world what had happened to us. I talked about the flags we made, the pride we had in our country, and how Big Tech had tried to silence us. I shared the story of how Shopify and Facebook had canceled our business, how we'd been left with no way to reach our customers, and how we were fighting back.

The response was immediate. Orders started pouring in from people who had seen the interview, people who believed in what we were doing and wanted to support us. In a single night, we received more orders than we'd had in months. It was overwhelming—in the best possible way.

But more than the orders, it was the confirmation that we were on the right path. That God had heard us, and He wasn't done with us yet. We weren't alone in this fight. And as long as we had faith, there was a way forward.

That phone call from Newsmax wasn't just a lifeline for our business—it was a sign that we were exactly where we were supposed to be. It gave us the strength to keep fighting, to keep pushing forward, even when it seemed like everything was against us.

From that point on, every time we hit a roadblock, we remembered that moment. We remembered the prayer, the phone call, and the peace that came with knowing that God had our backs. No matter how hard things got, we knew we weren't alone.

We had been tested, but we had also been blessed.

My Thoughts and Reflections:
That prayer marked a turning point for us. It wasn't just a moment of asking for help—it was a moment of surrender. We handed over the reins to God, trusting that He would show us the way. And He did. From that day forward, I knew we weren't alone in this fight. Every challenge, every setback, was just another step on the path He had laid out for us. Faith isn't just about believing when things are easy—it's about holding on when things are falling apart. And in that moment, when everything seemed lost, we found strength through prayer.

*"You just have to have faith
and trust in His timing."*

Chapter 10:
Canceled Round Two
(PayPal)

Just when we thought things were finally turning around after the Newsmax interview, we were hit with another crushing blow. This one was from PayPal, and it wasn't just an inconvenience—it was a full-blown financial disaster. If Shopify and Facebook cutting off our sales had been a gut punch, PayPal freezing our funds was like having the ground ripped out from under us.

It started the morning after the Newsmax interview. The interview had gone better than we could have imagined—orders were pouring in, and for the first time in months, we felt like we had a chance to get our business back on track. We woke up to hundreds of new orders, and it seemed like the hard times were finally behind us.

But that sense of relief didn't last long.

I went to place an order for the materials we needed to fulfill all those new sales—wood, paint, shipping supplies—but when I tried to use the PayPal debit card, it was declined. I thought there must've been some mistake, so I checked the account online. That's when I saw it: every single cent of our money had been frozen.

Everything we had made from the flood of new orders after the Newsmax interview—was locked up. PayPal had put a hold on all our funds with no warning, no explanation. I was furious. How could this be happening? We had just gotten a lifeline, and now PayPal had cut it off before we could even take a breath.

I immediately contacted PayPal's customer service, thinking there must have been some kind of error. Surely this was just a misunderstanding that could be cleared up quickly. But what I got from PayPal blew my mind.

We were told specifically by PayPal's customer service representative named "Scotty" and said this exactly.... "We froze your account because you have a 'shady' business, and we don't think you will be in business very much longer"! The tone he said this in was so vindictive and cruel that it made Ginger cry. I then jumped on the call and said, "So you are shutting down our business".

Scotty went on to say. "No, Don't worry, you can still take orders, and PayPal will charge the money and it will be frozen for 180 days, when we determine, what we want to do." I Said... "So we will get our money back in 180 days?" Scotty said... "No, that's when we will decide what we want to do." And then he laughed!

At first, I was angry. Then, I was scared. The reality of what PayPal's actions meant for our family started to sink in. That money wasn't just numbers on a screen—it was our ability to pay for the materials we needed to fulfill orders. It was our ability to pay our bills, to buy groceries, to keep the lights on.

Without access to those funds, we were stuck. We couldn't fulfill the new orders, which meant we couldn't bring in more money. And with our cash flow frozen, there was no way to keep the business running. The nightmare was happening all over again. We had been given a second chance after the Newsmax interview, and now it was slipping through our fingers.

The financial strain was immediate. We had been scraping by as it was, stretching every dollar, cutting back on everything we could. But this—this was different. This wasn't just a bad month or a slow quarter. This was our entire livelihood being held hostage by a corporation that couldn't care less about the people on the other side of the screen.

I remember sitting down with Ginger, trying to figure out how we were going to make it through the next few weeks. The weight of it all was crushing. We had orders piling up, but no way to fulfill them. Customers were starting to ask questions, wondering why their orders were delayed, and we didn't have any good answers for them.

It wasn't just about the business anymore. It was about our family. The stress of not knowing how we were going to pay for basic necessities was overwhelming. We had to start making tough decisions—decisions no family should have to make. We rationed food, put off doctor's appointments, and cut out anything that wasn't absolutely essential. Every day was a balancing act of trying to keep the business alive while keeping our family afloat.

For months, we were stuck in limbo.

PayPal had our money, and there was nothing we could do to get it back. I contacted them again and again, hoping to find someone who would actually listen, someone who would understand the impact this was having on us. But every time, I got the same response: "Freeze is a result of a review that we've already completed, and we will review the account again in 180 days."

All I could think was, "that's it, GAME OVER, NO OTHER OPTION!" It felt like a never-ending cycle of frustration and helplessness. Every time I saw the balance in that frozen PayPal account, it was a reminder of how powerless we were. PayPal held all the cards, and we were left to wait, with no idea when—or if—they would release our money.

Months passed, and the situation didn't improve.

The holidays came and went, and instead of celebrating with our family, we were worried about how we were going to get through the next month. The orders from the Newsmax interview had been our lifeline, but now, with PayPal keeping the funds, it felt like we were drowning all over again.

My Thoughts and Reflections:
Of all the challenges we faced, PayPal freezing our funds was the most devastating. When they locked our money, it wasn't just an inconvenience—it nearly destroyed our business. That money was what we needed to fulfill orders, pay for supplies, and keep our family afloat. Without it, we were paralyzed. The frustration of trying to get answers from PayPal was maddening. Their cold, automated responses offered no timeline, no solutions, just a vague "shady" label that left us in financial limbo for months.

The impact on our family was immediate and painful. We had to make hard decisions—what bills could be put off, what expenses we could cut back on, and how to keep the business alive with no cash flow. The stress of not knowing when, or if, we'd ever get our money back was overwhelming. It wasn't just about the business anymore—it was about survival. We were doing everything we could just to get by, but it felt like PayPal was holding our future hostage.

Looking back, I still feel anger at how easily a corporation like PayPal can crush a small business without consequence. But I'm proud of how we fought through it. We didn't give up, and we came out stronger. It taught me that no matter how powerful the opposition, standing your ground and fighting back is always worth it.

Chapter 11:
The Center for American Liberty

By the time PayPal had held our funds for months, we were feeling completely isolated, with no clear path forward. The frustration was mounting every day, knowing that the money we'd worked so hard for—money we desperately needed—was frozen, and there was seemingly no way to get it back. We were a small family business, and PayPal was a giant corporation with all the power. It felt like we were screaming into the void, unheard and unsupported.

Then, something extraordinary happened. Just when we were beginning to feel like there was no hope left, Harmeet Dhillon reached out to us. I'll never forget that moment. I immediately felt that Harmeet being on our path was God continuing to answer our prayer.

Harmeet, a high-profile attorney and founder of the Center for American Liberty, had heard about our story and wanted to help. It was like a lifeline had been thrown to us at the exact moment we needed it most.

Up until then, we had been fighting this battle alone. But suddenly, we had someone in our corner—someone with the knowledge, the resources, and the determination to take on a giant like PayPal.

Mark Meuser, the lead attorney on our case, became my main point of contact throughout this intense journey. Mark's approach to the law is both fair and diplomatic, but when he's fighting for others, he transforms into an absolute dog in the fight. His dedication to helping others extends beyond the courtroom. When Mark found out we were struggling to afford groceries and that our children were going to bed hungry and attending school with half-packed lunches due to PayPal withholding over $100,000 of our funds, he showed his incredible generosity. Mark bought a $2,000 flag from us, allowing us to put food on the table and catch up on some overdue bills. Remarkably, he even let us deliver the flag nine months later after we'd managed to fulfill other outstanding orders.

Additionally, I want to extend a heartfelt thank you to Bill Essayli and Mark Trammell. They were the first lawyers who listened to our story and took it to Harmeet Dhillon, setting the wheels in motion for the legal battle that would ultimately restore hope to our family.

Harmeet and the team at the Center for American Liberty didn't just see us as another case—they saw us as a family, as a small business being unfairly crushed by a powerful corporation. They believed in what we were fighting for, and more importantly, they believed that we could win.

The Center for American Liberty is an organization dedicated to protecting the constitutional rights of Americans, particularly those who are being silenced or oppressed by powerful institutions like Big Tech. They had taken on cases involving free speech, religious liberty, and, in our case, the right to operate a business without being unfairly targeted or censored.

When Harmeet and her team agreed to take on our case, we felt an enormous sense of relief. We didn't have the financial means to hire a lawyer, let alone someone as well-known and respected as Harmeet. But the Center for American Liberty took us on pro bono. They didn't want money; they wanted justice. They believed that what PayPal was doing was wrong, and they were determined to hold them accountable.

For months, we had been stuck in a cycle of emails and phone calls with PayPal, getting nowhere. They kept making excuses, stalling, and offering no real solutions. But the moment the Center for American Liberty got involved, the dynamic shifted. Suddenly, PayPal wasn't dealing with just a small business owner—they were dealing with a legal powerhouse, an organization that knew the law and wasn't afraid to go head-to-head with a corporate giant.

Harmeet Dhillon didn't waste any time. She and her team filed legal challenges against PayPal, demanding that they release the funds they were holding hostage. It was a long and grueling process, with PayPal dragging their feet at every turn. They didn't want to give up the money, and they certainly didn't want to admit any wrongdoing. But Harmeet wasn't backing down, and neither were we.

Throughout the legal battle, the Center for American Liberty kept us informed every step of the way. They were transparent, dedicated, and tireless in their efforts to get justice for us. More than anything, they gave us hope. For the first time in months, we felt like we had a real chance of getting our money back and holding PayPal accountable for their actions.

The fight wasn't easy. PayPal didn't back down without a fight. But with the Center for American Liberty on our side, we finally had the resources and the support we needed to stand our ground. Harmeet's legal expertise, combined with the unwavering determination of Mark Meuser and the entire team, turned the tide in our favor.

After months of legal wrangling, PayPal finally relented. They returned the money they had been holding for nearly a year. Even then, they tried to get us to sign a non-disclosure agreement, hoping we would quietly accept the money and go away. The Center for American Liberty DID NOT advise us to refuse the NDA! They simply laid out my options and made it clear that if I signed it, I would never be able to publicly mention what PayPal did to us, making our story impossible to be effective in fighting for change!

PayPal did NOT relent at all! Mark and Harmeet had to force them to release every single cent to us! And PayPal still held almost $11,000, and used that to what "felt like" extort us with it by demanding a NDA. And it would need to be signed for us to get that last 11K back. Apparently that's what's called "legal negotiation", yet it just didn't feel right to us.

Looking back, I realize that we wouldn't have been able to fight this battle on our own. The power imbalance between us and PayPal was just too great. But with the Center for American Liberty on our side, we had a fighting chance—and we won.

More than just winning this part of the legal battle, though, the Center for American Liberty gave us something even more valuable: hope. They showed us that even when the odds are stacked against you, even when it feels like you're fighting an unwinnable fight, there are people out there who will stand with you. They reminded us that justice is worth fighting for, and that no matter how big the opponent, the truth will always prevail.

In the end, the fight with PayPal wasn't just about money—it was about standing up for what was right. And thanks to Harmeet Dhillon and the Center for American Liberty, we were able to do just that.

My Thoughts and Reflections:
There are moments in life when you realize just how much of a difference one person—or one organization—can make. For us, that moment came when Harmeet Dhillon and the Center for American Liberty stepped in to help. Up until that point, we had been fighting what felt like a losing battle. PayPal had frozen our funds, and no matter how many emails, phone calls, or pleas for help we sent their way, nothing changed. It felt like we were shouting into the void, powerless against a giant corporation that could take away our livelihood without a second thought.

But when the Center for American Liberty got involved, everything changed. Suddenly, we weren't just a small family business trying to take on Big Tech. We had allies—people who understood the law, who had the experience and resources to take on a company like PayPal, and who believed in what we were fighting for. Harmeet Dhillon didn't just offer us legal advice; she offered us hope.

I can't overstate what that meant to us. When you're in the middle of a battle like the one we were fighting, it's easy to feel overwhelmed, isolated, and defeated. Every day, we were waking up to the reality that PayPal still had our money and that our ability to run our business was being held hostage. It was terrifying. We had bills to pay, orders to fulfill, and a family to take care of, but without access to those funds, everything felt like it was slipping away. We had been forced to ration everything—from food to supplies—just to keep going.

I remember the first conversation we had with Harmeet. She didn't just talk about legal strategy—she listened to our story. She wanted to understand not just the legalities of the case, but the human toll it had taken on us. That's what set her and the Center for American Liberty apart. They didn't see us as just another case; they saw us as real people whose lives and livelihoods had been upended by corporate overreach.

From the moment they took on our case, everything felt different. For the first time in months, we felt like we had a fighting chance. PayPal, with all its money and power, no longer seemed invincible. The Center for American Liberty leveled the playing field. They were relentless in their pursuit of justice, filing legal challenges and standing up to PayPal's lawyers with a fierce determination that we could never have managed on our own.

Harmeet Dhillon and her team were exactly what we needed in that moment. They gave us back our voice when PayPal had tried to silence us. They gave us back our hope when we were on the verge of losing everything. And, most importantly, they gave us back our ability to fight.

But the Center for American Liberty didn't just win us a legal victory. They helped us see the bigger picture. Our battle with PayPal wasn't just about getting our money back. It was about standing up to a system where companies like PayPal can play by their own rules, with little regard for the people whose lives they affect. The fight wasn't just about us—it was about every small business out there that had been bullied by Big Tech, every entrepreneur who had been forced to live in fear of being deplatformed or financially crippled without warning.

Without the Center for American Liberty, we would have lost everything. But because of them, we didn't just survive—we came out stronger. They reminded us that no matter how big the corporation or how daunting the challenge, there is always a way to fight back. There are always people out there who will stand with you, who will help you fight for what's right.

We are still working with The Center for American Liberty to bring our case to its final conclusion at the right time, where we will receive a proper apology and be compensated fairly for the lost income, damage to our reputation, damage to our credit, damage to our marriage, and the stress our kids were forced to endure over the 311 day HELL we were unnecessarily put through!

Chapter 12:
Rebuilding with The Media
& Strategic Partners

The relentless battle against cancel culture, platform shutdowns, and financial blockades left Ginger and me drained, facing a bleak future for our business. Despite our efforts to adapt and reach out to customers, everything we built seemed on the verge of collapse. One night, desperate for a breakthrough, we prayed, asking for a path forward that would let us keep fighting without compromising our values. The very next morning, that prayer was answered in ways we could never have anticipated.

It started with a call from Newsmax. Their team had come across our story, and they wanted us to share our experience. That night, I joined Rob Schmitt on his show, *Rob Schmitt Tonight*, where I opened up about our struggles with big tech censorship, the targeting of our patriotic product line, and the financial stranglehold companies like PayPal had on us. Rob's genuine interest and support provided a platform to speak out against the unjust obstacles that were holding us back. After that interview aired, we received a wave of orders and messages of support, reminding us that many people still cared about the principles of free enterprise and shared our love for this country. It was a much-needed ray of hope.

However, just as things started to turn around, PayPal still refused to release our money, and to make matters worse, they demanded we sign a non-disclosure agreement to access our last $11,000, essentially silencing us from ever sharing our story. That offer just made us feel as if we were being extorted with our own money. But going up against a financial giant like PayPal felt impossible.

This was when a new ally stepped in. I reached out to former Congressman Sean Duffy, now a host at Fox News. Sean immediately understood the severity of our situation and took action, connecting us with his wife, Rachel Campos-Duffy, a co-host on *Fox & Friends*. They arranged for me to appear on *Fox & Friends*, where I could share the full scope of our struggle. The experience was surreal—Sean, Rachel, and the Fox News team showed us unwavering support, letting us highlight how big tech and financial giants were using their influence to control and silence small businesses. Just hours after that interview aired, PayPal released our funds, ending a 311-day ordeal. Sean and Rachel's support was instrumental in making that happen, proving the power of standing together against unjust systems.

Our financial stability started to recover, but Christina Warner of Public Square who had become one of our trusted allies, knew we needed more than a temporary fix. She encouraged us to seek out strategic partners that aligned with our mission and values, helping us avoid the pitfalls of platforms that could turn against us.

Christina was incredibly helpful, supportive and crucial to us learning the value of Strategic Partnerships! Christina asked us to join the movement she and her team of pioneers were starting at Public Square, guaranteeing me that we would always be valued there and would **NEVER** be canceled! While at the time, Public Square was not even launched in Tennessee, I was allowed in and am proud that I was the very first person in Tennessee to join Public Squares "Parallel Economy" movement, and have been one of their original and most visible advocates. I am extremely proud to be 4 in line in a incredible group of men who have mentioned Public Square on National TV, behind Public Squares CEO Michael Seifert, Donald Trump Jr. who sit on their board and Tucker Carlson who is their biggest advocate. I could not say that if not for Christina Werner's reaching out to me in one of our darkest times and bringing me into the Public Square family! Public Square became our first Strategic Partner, and I believe that today they are our most loyal and loudest supporter!

Thomas Troyer, the owner of Second Amendment Processing, a credit card processor that promised fair, reliable service without political bias. Thomas saw us on Fox News! And reached out to us after he saw what PayPal had done and offered to process our credit cards for a better rate and promised that he would make sure that we would never have our money taken from us again!

With the help of Christina, Rob Schmitt, Sean, and Rachel, we were able to rebuild stronger than before. The support of Newsmax and *Fox & Friends* brought invaluable visibility to our story, proving that the right allies can make all the difference. We found resilience through faith, family, and partnerships with those who truly understood and supported our cause.

My Thoughts and Reflections:
The combined power of Newsmax and Fox News gave us more than a platform—they gave us a lifeline. Appearing on *Rob Schmitt Tonight* and *Fox & Friends* wasn't just about publicity; it was a pivotal moment that allowed us to

stand up against the giants trying to silence us. Through these appearances, we found allies who understood our struggle and were willing to lend their voices to help us fight back. Rob Schmitt, Sean Duffy, and Rachel Campos-Duffy weren't just television hosts; they were advocates who believed in the principles we were defending.

These moments weren't only about reclaiming what was ours—they were about justice and faith. Christina Warner's guidance to align with strategic partners who shared our values brought us Second Amendment Processing, a partner that, unlike PayPal, valued our freedom to operate without interference. God placed each of these individuals in our path at precisely the right time, guiding us step by step.

Looking back, I can see that every setback we faced had a purpose. When we felt surrounded by obstacles, the right help appeared, reminding us that faith was our anchor. This journey has shown us that when you're on the right path, obstacles will come, but so will the support you need to overcome them. All you have to do is trust, have faith, and keep fighting.

*"Every step of the way,
God was guiding us,
putting the right people in our path
at the right time."*

Chapter 13:
The Tennessee Legislature

After fighting our way through the seemingly endless battles with Shopify, Facebook, and PayPal, one thing became clear: what we had experienced wasn't just an isolated incident. Small businesses like ours were increasingly finding themselves at the mercy of Big Tech companies that could shut them down, freeze their funds, or block their advertisements without any real accountability. It wasn't just a business problem; it was a systemic issue that needed to be addressed at a higher level.

That's when we got the call from Monty Fritts, a local Tennessee state legislator who had been following our story. He knew what we had gone through—how Shopify had shut down our bestselling products, how Facebook had blocked our ads, and how PayPal had nearly destroyed us by freezing our funds. But most importantly, he knew that our story wasn't unique. More and more small business owners were being silenced and deplatformed by Big Tech, and he wanted to do something about it.

Monty invited us to testify before the Tennessee legislature as part of a push to create new laws that would protect small businesses from the overreach of companies like PayPal, Facebook, and Shopify. It was a chance not just to tell our story, but to help influence real change— change that could protect others from going through the nightmare we had experienced.

When we arrived at the state capitol in Nashville, the weight of what we were doing really sank in. This wasn't just about us anymore. We were standing up for every small business that had been pushed around, every entrepreneur who had been silenced, and every family whose livelihood had been put in jeopardy by corporate giants. It was bigger than our own fight—it was about protecting the very foundation of free enterprise in America.

The day we testified was nerve-wracking. I'd never done anything like this before, and the stakes felt incredibly high. But we were ready. We had prepared our testimony carefully, laying out every detail of our experience with Big Tech's censorship and financial stranglehold. This was our chance to shine a light on the injustices we had faced and to show the legislators exactly how devastating it could be for small businesses when these tech companies were allowed to act with impunity.

As we sat in front of the legislative committee, I could feel the tension in the room. Some of the lawmakers were already familiar with our story, but others were hearing it for the first time. I could see the looks on their faces as we recounted the details—how Shopify had pulled our bestselling products without warning, how Facebook had blocked us from advertising because of a single customer's post, and how PayPal had held over $100,000 of our hard-earned money for nearly a year, crippling our ability to operate.

When we told them about PayPal's refusal to release our funds without us signing a non-disclosure agreement, you could feel the outrage in the room. These were lawmakers who understood small businesses, who knew what it was like to build something from the ground up, and they couldn't believe what we had been put through.

But it wasn't just about PayPal. It was about the bigger picture—the unchecked power of Big Tech companies that were increasingly acting as gatekeepers to the digital marketplace. These companies were making decisions that could make or break a small business, and they were doing it without any transparency or accountability. If we didn't stand up to them, this problem would only get worse.

I spoke about the emotional toll it had taken on our family, the financial strain we had endured, and the fear of losing everything we had worked so hard to build. But more than that, I spoke about the need for change. Small businesses shouldn't have to live in fear of being canceled without warning, without reason, and without recourse.

After we finished our testimony, there was a moment of silence. Then, one of the legislators leaned forward and said, "This has to stop." It was a powerful moment—one that made me realize that we weren't just telling our story; we were helping to shape the future for other small businesses across the state and potentially the country.

The legislators asked us questions about the specifics of what had happened, how it had affected our ability to operate, and what kind of protections we thought small businesses needed. We talked about the importance of transparency—how companies like PayPal, Facebook, and Shopify should be required to explain their actions, and how there needed to be a clear process for businesses to challenge these decisions.

We also discussed the need for legal protections that would prevent Big Tech from using their platforms to financially cripple businesses, as PayPal had done to us. No business should have to wait 311 days to access the money it has earned, and no company should be able to hold funds hostage without facing legal consequences.

By the time we left the hearing, I felt a sense of accomplishment, but also a renewed sense of responsibility. Testifying before the legislature wasn't the end of our fight—it was just the beginning. The legislative process would take time, and there were no guarantees that the laws we were advocating for would pass. But we had taken the first step, and that was what mattered.

The Tennessee legislature's response to our testimony gave us hope. Lawmakers like Monty Fritts were committed to protecting small businesses and ensuring that what happened to us wouldn't happen to others. And while we knew there was a long road ahead, we were determined to keep fighting—not just for ourselves, but for every entrepreneur who had been silenced, deplatformed, or financially crippled by Big Tech.

Our testimony was a reminder that the power of a small business isn't just in the products it sells or the services it offers—it's in the people behind it, the community it supports, and the principles it stands for. And in that moment, standing before the Tennessee legislature, we knew we weren't just fighting for our business. We were fighting for the rights of every small business owner who had been pushed to the brink by forces beyond their control.

This fight wasn't over. But now, with the support of lawmakers who understood the stakes, we were no longer alone.

My Thoughts and Reflections:
Testifying before the Tennessee legislature was one of the most surreal and humbling experiences of my life. When I started *Your American Flag Store*, I never imagined that I would one day be sitting in front of lawmakers, sharing the story of how my family's business had been nearly destroyed by the unchecked power of Big Tech. I wasn't a politician or a public speaker—I was just a small business owner who had built something out of passion and hard work. And yet, there I was, telling my story to people who had the power to make real, lasting change.

The decision to testify wasn't easy. For months, we had been in survival mode—fighting to keep our business afloat, scrambling to pay bills, and trying to navigate a system that seemed rigged against us. The idea of going before a legislative body and speaking about our experiences felt intimidating, to say the least. But as I sat there in front of those lawmakers, I realized that this wasn't just about us anymore. This was about standing up for every small business owner who had been silenced, deplatformed, or financially crippled by corporations that held all the cards.

The day I testified, I was struck by how different our world is from the one I thought I knew. When we started this business, we believed in the American Dream—that if you worked hard, treated your customers right, and provided a good product, you could succeed. But as we learned, that dream can quickly turn into a nightmare when powerful companies like PayPal, Shopify, and Facebook decide to shut you down without warning or reason. They don't care about the human cost, the families affected, or the livelihoods destroyed. To them, we were just numbers—faceless accounts they could cut off with the flick of a switch.

That's why it was so important for me to share our story. It wasn't about revenge or seeking pity—it was about accountability. These companies needed to be held responsible for their actions, and I wanted the lawmakers to understand that what happened to us could happen to anyone. If they didn't act to protect small businesses, the cycle of censorship and financial ruin would continue unchecked.

As I testified, I thought about all the other small business owners who might be too afraid to speak up. I thought about the entrepreneurs who had been canceled but didn't have the resources or the platform to fight back. I thought about how easily we could have been silenced if we hadn't found allies like Harmeet Dhillon and the Center for American Liberty. It became clear to me that this fight wasn't just ours—it was a fight for the future of free enterprise.

When one of the lawmakers leaned forward and said, "This has to stop," it felt like validation—not just for us, but for everyone who had been wronged by these tech giants. It was a reminder that our voices do matter, that speaking up can make a difference, and that change is possible if we're willing to fight for it.

But the experience also taught me something else: change doesn't happen overnight. Testifying before the legislature was just the first step. The laws we were advocating for would take time to pass, and there would be opposition along the way. But for the first time in a long time, I felt hopeful. I felt like we were part of something bigger, something that could make a real difference for small businesses across the country.

Looking back on that day, I'm proud that we took the stand we did. I'm proud that we didn't let fear or frustration silence us. And most of all, I'm proud that we fought not just for our business, but for the countless others who had been, or could be, in the same position.

The fight isn't over. But now, we're no longer fighting alone. With lawmakers like Monty Fritts on our side and with the support of organizations like the Center for American Liberty, we're pushing back against a system that has gone unchecked for far too long. And we won't stop until small businesses are given the protections they deserve.

At the end of the day, this experience has reminded me of something fundamental: the American Dream isn't about wealth or success. It's about freedom—the freedom to build, to create, to speak, and to stand up for what's right. And that's something worth fighting for.

Chapter 14:
Bouncing Back

Life has a way of knocking you down when you least expect it. We were riding high, putting our American flags out there, sharing a message of pride and patriotism, and connecting with people who love this country.

But then, without warning, Facebook decided to demonetize our page, citing vague "community standards." Suddenly, our income stream was cut off, all because our handcrafted American flags didn't fit their "standards."

These big tech companies claim to support free expression, but when it doesn't align with their vision, they don't hesitate to pull the plug.

They promote "community" and "inclusion," but when you don't fit their narrative, they turn their backs. We didn't sit around feeling sorry for ourselves, though.

You can take away a source of income, but you can't take away our drive.

So, we fought back. We adapted and found new avenues to keep going. We connected with people who understood our mission, finding new platforms and resources that aligned with our values. The support from our customers was overwhelming—they saw through the censorship and backed us even more fiercely.

Through this, we grew stronger, learning the resilience it takes to keep moving forward, no matter what obstacles are thrown our way.

This experience reminded me of a crucial truth: adversity will come, and people may try to shut you down, but true strength comes from getting back up, bigger and stronger than before.

My Thoughts and Reflections:

You know, life has this way of testing you—pushing you to the edge and seeing what you're made of. Getting hit by Facebook's demonetization was just one of those moments.

But here's what I've come to realize: You can't control what happens to you, but you can control how you respond.

That's where real strength comes from.

This journey has shown me that resilience, grit, and faith in what you believe are more powerful than any algorithm or corporate decision. When they tried to shut us down, we stood taller. We got creative. We leaned on our supporters and, most importantly, we didn't let a setback define us.

We proved that the American spirit is more than just a concept—it's a living, breathing force that rises up in the face of adversity. So, to anyone reading this who's been knocked down, remember this: The road ahead might not be easy, but if you stay true to your purpose and refuse to give up, you'll find a way.

If we can bounce back bigger and better, so can you.

Cancel culture might try, but it can't take away your drive, your passion, or your faith in what you're building. And that's what I want everyone to take away from this—keep pushing forward and know that as long as you believe in yourself and what you stand for, you're already uncanceled.

"Life will knock you down,
no doubt about it.
But the real test is how you bounce back.
It's not about staying down—
it's about rising stronger and
smarter every single time."

Chapter 15:
Justice

After months of battling Big Tech, from PayPal holding our money hostage to Facebook and Shopify canceling our ability to do business, we finally started to see some victories. But the more we pushed back, the more I realized that our fight wasn't just about *Your American Flag Store*—it was about something much bigger. It wasn't just about getting our money back or making sure our business survived. It was about making sure this kind of thing didn't happen to other small business owners across the country.

The truth is, the system is set up to favor the giants—Facebook, PayPal, Shopify—and it became clear that if we wanted real justice, we needed to change the laws. These companies had more money than we could ever dream of, political connections that ran deep, and the legal system on their side.

But what they didn't have was our story, our voice, and the truth about how they were hurting small businesses like ours.

One of the key moments in this fight came when Monty Fritts entered the picture. Monty was a local guy running for office in Tennessee, and he had been following our story closely. He wasn't just a politician—he was a Marine Corps veteran and a true patriot. After serving his country and working at Y-12 in Oak Ridge, Tennessee, Monty had re-enlisted after 9/11 to help the younger soldiers in combat. When he heard what Big Tech had done to our family, Monty was outraged, and he made it clear that he wanted to do something about it.

After Monty won his election, he wasted no time. He called me right away, telling me that we were going to work on legislation to make sure what happened to us wouldn't happen to anyone else. About a year later, I found myself testifying in front of the Tennessee legislature, sharing our story—how PayPal had nearly starved our family by withholding our money, how my wife had to ration food, how my daughter missed orthodontic appointments, and how my son didn't get new school clothes. I talked about skipping meals so there was enough for the kids.

Monty took this personally, and he was determined to push the legislation forward.

On the day of the vote, I was hopeful that justice was finally within reach. Monty had lined up the votes, and I was ready to see real change happen. But when I arrived in Nashville, Monty met me in the hallway with bad news—PayPal had sent in lobbyists to fight against the bill, and they had managed to sway enough people that we didn't have the votes anymore. It was a gut punch, but Monty didn't give up. He told me to go into that room, tell my story, and let the chips fall where they may.

I brought Max and Evie with me that day because I wanted the legislators to see the faces of the kids who had been impacted by PayPal's actions. This wasn't just about money—it was about the real, human consequences of what these corporations were doing.

I testified, sharing everything we had been through, and the response blew me away.

Lawmakers from both sides of the aisle came up to me afterward, offering support, some even giving me hugs. There were still a few who sat there with their arms crossed, unwilling to budge, but overall, it was clear that our story had hit home.

That legislation—Tennessee House Bill 846—is now making its way through the system. Monty Fritts wrote it, Senator Ken Yeager is sponsoring it, and now a new ally has joined the fight—Congressman Tim Burchett. Tim has committed to taking this battle to the federal level, making sure that what happened to us won't happen to other small business owners across the country. This bill is an anti-debanking law, designed to protect people from being deliberately targeted and bankrupted by big corporations.

The fight isn't over, but we're making progress. What started as a local issue is now being taken to the national stage, and we're determined to see it through. Congressman Burchett has been a strong advocate, and next week, I'm scheduled to meet with Matt Gaetz to discuss further steps.

We're building momentum, and with each new supporter, it feels like justice is finally within reach.

My Thoughts and Reflections:

Justice doesn't always come quickly, and it rarely comes easily. But the fight for justice is one worth pursuing, no matter how long it takes. PayPal, Facebook, and Shopify may have more money and influence, but they don't have the truth on their side. Our story, and the stories of countless others, will be the driving force behind real change. This battle is far from over, but I believe in what we're doing. We're not just fighting for ourselves—we're fighting for every small business owner who has been pushed around by Big Tech, for every family who has been starved out by corporate greed. Real justice means standing up, speaking out, and pushing for laws that protect the people, not just the corporations. And with the help of people like Monty Fritts, Senator Ken Yeager, Tim Burchett, and soon Matt Gaetz, we're getting closer to making that a reality.

"Cancel culture might try,
but it can't crush the American spirit.
We're living proof of that."

Chapter 16: Conclusion:
The Fight for Legacy and Freedom

As I look back on the journey that brought us here, one thing is clear: this has always been about more than just a business. It's been about family, faith, and standing up for what we believe in. When we started *Your American Flag Store*, we had no idea it would turn into a fight against some of the biggest corporations in the world—companies that tried to cancel us, silence us, and erase the very values we hold dear.

But we never gave up.

We couldn't.

Because giving up meant letting go of everything we worked for—our livelihood, our pride, our belief in the American dream. This business started with a simple idea from our son, Max, but it grew into something much larger than any of us ever imagined. It became a symbol of resilience, a testament to the power of truth and tenacity in the face of adversity.

Through every challenge—whether it was being deplatformed by Big Tech or fighting to get back the money PayPal wrongfully held from us—we learned that freedom is never guaranteed.

You have to fight for it.

You have to protect it.

And sometimes, you have to defend it against forces much bigger than yourself.

But when you do, when you refuse to back down, that's when you truly embody the spirit of free enterprise and the American dream.

This book isn't just a record of the struggles we've faced as a family—it's a call to action for every entrepreneur, every patriot, every individual who believes in the power of hard work and the freedom to pursue their dreams. It's a reminder that no matter how powerful the opposition, there's always a way to fight back. And in that fight, we find our purpose, our strength, and our legacy.

The road ahead isn't always easy.

There will always be obstacles.

There will always be those who try to shut you down, to tell you that you don't belong, to make you feel small. But if there's one thing we've learned, it's this: as long as you stay true to who you are, as long as you fight for what's right, you can never truly be canceled.

Our story is far from over.

We will continue to stand up for free enterprise, for family, and for the freedom to create a life we're proud of. And with every flag we make, with every story we tell, we are building a legacy—a legacy of resilience, of courage, and of unshakeable belief in the American dream.

Because in the end, it's not just about surviving. It's about thriving.

It's about making sure that the next generation—our children, and their children—know what it means to stand up for what's right. That's our legacy. And that's what we're fighting for.

My Final Reflection: The journey of *Your American Flag Store* has been about far more than building a business. It has been about standing firm in the face of adversity, embracing resilience, and staying true to the values that matter most—family, freedom, and the American dream. What we've faced is not unique. Entrepreneurs across the country are battling their own versions of censorship, cancel culture, and the challenges of modern-day business. But our story is proof that, no matter how powerful the opposition, there is always a way to rise above it.

The lessons we've learned along the way have been hard-fought. We've learned that success doesn't come without sacrifice, and that building something meaningful often requires weathering storms you never saw coming. But we've also learned that the strength to keep going comes from the people who stand with you—your family, your community, and the allies you gain along the way. It is this collective spirit of resilience that makes us unstoppable.

In the end, this journey is about more than just flags or business. It's about creating a lasting legacy—one that shows future generations that they can fight back when the world tries to silence them. It's about proving that with faith, courage, and determination, no one can take away what you've built.

The road to preserving free enterprise and the American dream isn't easy, but it's one worth traveling. And for us, the fight continues—not just for ourselves, but for every small business owner who dares to dream. Because the legacy we leave behind is not just a testament to what we've overcome, but a beacon for those who will follow in our footsteps.

"Adversity isn't the end of your journey
—it's a turning point."

*"Thank you for reading our stories.
It's been my pleasure sharing them with you."*

Special Thanks

As I look back on the journey that has led to this book, there's a profound sense of gratitude that fills me. This story, our story, wouldn't be here without the remarkable people who walked with us through the struggles, the successes, and the surprises. So many have offered their support, encouragement, and inspiration along the way, and each one has left an indelible mark on this journey.

After my wife and I said our prayer, the next morning God began putting people on the path we asked him to show us. Each of these people has had a role in our company staying open, our family staying together, our story being told, or our experience having a purpose greater than ourselves. For their contribution we will be forever grateful.

Tim Reiland, Derek Utley, Christopher Ruddy,
Harmeet Dhillon, Chris Knowles, Mark Meuser,
Loren Emory, Mark Trammell, Alison Maloni, Bill Essayli,
Rob Finnerty, Mason Winters, Rob Schmitt, Alex Avetoom,
Tom Baseli, Sean Duffy, Rob Sigg, Rachael Campos Duffy,
Don Neuen, Amos Benjamin, Donna Fiducia, Monty Fritts,
Ed Henry, Tim Burchett, Christina Werner, Mike Ralston,
Robbie Jones, Stacy Washington, Ken Nuss,
Max & Diane Winters, Eugene Honrath, Dan Tanner,
Justin & Sean Moon, Gregg Noll, Gerry Letendre,
Shannon Hutto, Suri Khar,
& John Thomas Patton.

Also, thanks to the media and strategic partners...

NEWSMAX, FOX NEWS,
Real America's Voice, Public Square,
The Center for American Liberty, Tannerite,
Kahr Arms, 2nd Amendment Processing, Titan 3D,
& Smokey Mountain Wood Products

And to **Rob Anspach** for taking such an in-depth look into me and my family's experience, making it possible to share it with you.

Thank you to all our friends, supporters, and customers who shared our mission, believed in our message, and rallied around us in our fight for free enterprise and the American Dream. You gave us strength when we needed it most, and you've been the heartbeat of our business.

Thank you to everyone who's been part of this journey. This book is a tribute to all of you who believed in us. It's a reminder that no matter the obstacles, no matter who tries to silence you, truth and resilience will always have the last word.

Lastly, to Big Tech itself—though you tried to cancel us, you inadvertently brought this story to life. By opposing us, by testing our resolve, you helped fuel our determination to keep going, to keep creating, and to keep standing up for what we believe in. Without that struggle, we wouldn't have discovered our strength, our purpose, or this mission we're now so committed to.

Resources

Newsmax – Media platform that aired James Staake's story and boosted support for his business. https://www.newsmax.com

Fox News – A media platform that airs stories focused on issues related to free enterprise and cancel culture. https://www.foxnews.com

Real America's Voice – Another media platform that highlights stories on American values and freedom of speech. https://americasvoice.news

Harmeet Dhillon – Lawyer from Dhillon Law Group who helped James Staake regain funds withheld by PayPal. https://www.dhillonlaw.com

Center for American Liberty – Provided legal support for James Staake against PayPal. https://libertycenter.org

Public Square – Platform that partners with and supports businesses like James Staake's in promoting freedom of speech and enterprise. https://www.publicsq.com

Derek Utley – X Strategies & Executive Producer of "Your American Family" www.xstrategies.com

Rob Anspach's E-Heroes Podcast – A platform where James Staake's story was shared and gained attention. https://e-heroes.anspachmedia.com

Monty Fritts – Tennessee Congressman who wrote Bill TN HB 846 https://www.fritts4tn32.com

Tim Burchett – U.S. Congressman supporting anti-cancel culture legislation. https://burchett.house.gov

Boot Campaign – a 501c3 non-profit corporation www.bootcampaign.org

Parabellum PR – Public relations support to fight cancel culture. https://parabellumpr.com

Freedom Fest – Event organized by Staake to celebrate his victory over cancel culture and raise awareness about small businesses being targeted. https://www.freedomfest.com

About James Staake

James Staake is a dedicated Christian carpenter, a skilled American flag maker, and a passionate defender of free enterprise and faith. Known for his meticulous craftsmanship, James founded **Your American Flag Store** after his young son's idea to handcraft wooden flags blossomed into a thriving business.

His flags are more than just symbols of patriotism—they reflect James' deep commitment to God, country, and family. James' journey gained national attention when Big Tech companies attempted to cancel his business for expressing his beliefs and values. Facebook and PayPal targeted him, freezing his business funds and restricting his ability to advertise. Rather than succumbing to the pressure, James turned this adversity into a mission.

Fueled by his faith, he fought back, not just for his business, but for the rights of all entrepreneurs facing similar challenges.

His story resonated across the country, appearing on platforms like **Newsmax** and **Rob Anspach's E-Heroes Podcast**. With the help of attorney **Harmeet Dhillon** and the **Center for American Liberty**, James successfully fought against cancel culture and reclaimed his business.

His efforts didn't stop there—James became a staunch advocate for free speech and individual rights in the digital age. He spearheaded the implementation of Anti-Cancel Culture Legislation in Tennessee, promoting protections for small businesses and individuals against unjust censorship.

Above all, James Staake is a devoted husband and father whose resilience and unwavering faith have transformed obstacles into opportunities for growth and advocacy. His story is not only one of entrepreneurial success, but of standing firm in one's beliefs, defending freedom, and creating a legacy rooted in faith and perseverance.

https://www.youramericanflagstore.com

The Staake Family

About Rob Anspach

Rob Anspach is a dynamic entrepreneur, marketing consultant, author, and podcast host who has dedicated over three decades to helping businesses build authority, craft legacies, and achieve long-term success.

 Rob is known for his no-nonsense, direct approach to marketing, often sharing his philosophies through what he calls "Rob-isms"—succinct, memorable principles that guide his clients in attracting high-value customers while avoiding low-hanging, problem-prone clients. His principles, like "The cheaper the client, the more hassles involved," have become well-known in entrepreneurial circles. Rob is particularly passionate about helping entrepreneurs realize their worth, encouraging them to charge what they're truly worth and create businesses that can stand the test of time.

In addition to his work with Anspach Media, Rob is the host of *E-Heroes Podcast*, where he interviews successful entrepreneurs and delves into topics like legacy, storytelling, and business authority. He is also the author of dozens of books, including the *Rob Versus* series, with the most popular title being *Rob Versus The Scammers*, where he humorously chronicles his efforts to waste the time of phone scammers. The series reflects Rob's sharp wit and penchant for storytelling, which he uses to connect with audiences both in writing and in person.

A key theme in Rob's work is legacy. He believes that most entrepreneurs fail to plan for the future, and his mission is to help businesses create lasting impacts that go beyond mere financial success. He frequently writes and speaks about the importance of legacy, noting that his own success stems from constantly thinking about how to ensure long-term value for his clients.

Rob's approach is rooted in relationship-building, as evidenced by his "friends first, client second" policy. This unique philosophy drives him to maintain strong connections with his clients even during difficult times, a value he feels is often lost in the competitive business world. Through Anspach Media, Rob has helped countless businesses refine their messaging, establish authority, and leave a lasting mark on their industries.

His dedication to both his craft and his clients has made him a sought-after consultant and trusted advisor for high-level businesses looking to scale while maintaining authenticity and a focus on legacy.

You can learn more by visiting www.AnspachMedia.com